Setting Up Stones

Applause for *Setting Up Stones*

"I wish we had had *Setting Up Stones* when we were raising our children. It's very insightful and full of grace—you do need a lot of that when you are raising little ones. Blessings on your project!"

—Fletch Wiley, Grammy Award winner, Dove Award winner, director of music;
Capital Church, McLean, Virginia

"*Setting Up Stones* is an authentic, practical, and insightful book. It is not just about family devotions. Instead it is an inspirational example of what a godly family should look like in the twenty-first century. Families at any stage of life can rejuvenate their spiritual and family relationships.

As a family physician, I see tremendous struggles in families, which cause mental, emotional, and physical illness. I know that incorporating the ideas in this book would greatly improve every aspect of health in families. I would recommend this to anyone who wants a more cohesive family and an atmosphere of worship in their home."

—Michael Newnam, MD;
Harvard Family Physicians, Tulsa, Oklahoma

"I think *Setting Up Stones* is for all parents trying to influence their kids in a healthy manner. The Singletons do a good job of offering hope and that hope will bring peace, comfort, and a host of other good stuff.

They describe an environment where worship is really an ongoing learning process, which is very refreshing. After reading this book, I am encouraged to pile up a few stones of my own in such a way that my family responds to who God is. Thanks for reminding me of the little things that matter."

—Byron Weathersbee, president;
Legacy Family Ministries, Waco, Texas

"In their book, *Setting Up Stones*, Greg and Martha Singleton have illustrated the truth with exercises and anecdotes that pattern excellent models of behavior. I would be pleased to recommend this book not only as an adult alternative Sunday School study, but also as an at-home study for families wanting better ways to practice their faith."

—Sanford Williams, certified family counselor, pastor of Christian education;
Trinity Church, San Antonio, Texas

Setting Up Stones

A Parent's Guide
to Making Your Home a Place of Worship

Martha and Greg Singleton

NEW HOPE
PUBLISHERS

Birmingham, Alabama

New Hope® Publishers
P. O. Box 12065
Birmingham, AL 35202-2065
www.newhopepublishers.com

New Hope Publishers is a division of WMU®.

Library of Congress Cataloging-in-Publication Data

Singleton, Martha, 1949-
  Setting up stones : a parent's guide to making your home a place of worship / Martha and Greg Singleton.
    p. cm.
  ISBN 978-1-59669-219-0 (sc)
  1. Family--Religious life. 2. Worship. I. Singleton, Greg, 1952- II. Title.
  BV200.S56 2008
  249--dc22

                    2008012900

All Scripture quotations, unless otherwise indicated, are taken from the HOLY BIBLE, NEW INTERNATIONAL VERSION®. NIV®. Copyright © 1973, 1978, 1984 by International Bible Society. Used by permission of Zondervan. All rights reserved.

Scripture quotations marked *The Message* are taken from *The Message* by Eugene H. Peterson. Copyright © 1993, 1994, 1995, 1996, 2000, 2001, 2002. Used by permission of NavPress Publishing Group.

Scripture quotations marked NKJV are taken from the New King James Version. Copyright © 1982 by Thomas Nelson, Inc. Used by permission. All rights reserved.

Scripture quotations marked NLT are taken from the *Holy Bible*, New Living Translation, copyright © 1996. Used by permission of Tyndale House Publishers, Inc., Wheaton, Illinois. All rights reserved.

Scripture quotations marked KJV are taken from The Holy Bible, King James Version.

Cover design by Birdsong Creative; www.birdsongcreative.com
Interior design by Sherry Hunt

ISBN-10: 1-59669-219-7
ISBN-13: 978-1-59669-219-0

N084142 • 1008 • 4M1

Table of Contents

In the midst of today's cultural noise, is there any way we can transform
our homes into places of worship?

Section One: Laying the Foundation

The stones placed in the Hebrews' dwellings were just as provocative as they
would be in our own living rooms.

God challenges us to break out of our little box and discover even more ways
to worship Him.

Worshipping God without knowing Him is like trying to describe chocolate cake
without ever having tasted it.

Make no mistake, our kids know when we're bluffing.

By deliberate and conscious design, we can use pop culture trends, events, and media
as teaching tools to direct our children to Christ and point out His activity in
today's world.

Whatever home looks like, it can be a place where God's presence dwells.

SECTION TWO: Building the Altar of Worship

Acknowledgments

God gave us a number of special people who helped us along the way.

Cheri Fuller, thank you for your encouragement and sound advice that pointed us in the right direction.

Fletch Wiley, thanks so much for sharing your insightful perspective on worship. Your music and your friendship through all these years have blessed our family.

Pastor Sanford Williams, Dr. Michael and Danelle Newnam, and Dr. Byron Weathersbee, your feedback was crucial, and we appreciate your time, honesty, and ideas. Even more, we appreciate all that each of you has been in our lives and the lives of our kids. We love you!

Les Stobbe, our agent, thank you for your efforts on our behalf, your invaluable guidance, and your prayers. You are a blessing to us.

Andrea Mullins, Jonathan Howe, Randy Bishop, Jean Baswell, Tina Atchenson, Joyce Dinkins, and the New Hope staff, what a privilege it is to work with you. The unity of purpose we sensed from the beginning is a joy and a strength.

To generations of our families before us, thank you for making the sacrifices that provided a foundation of faith and an atmosphere of worship.

Robbie, our son-in-law, your enthusiasm and affirmation provided great motivation. We're so thankful that God brought, in you, another worshipper to our family.

Annie and Matt, our children, thank you for letting us tell our stories about you! By your choices, you always made our home a place of joyful worship, and seeing you now use your lives as living stones that call others to God is a blessing beyond measure.

Introduction

Sometimes I feel like a ringmaster in a three-ring circus."

That's how a frustrated father once described to us his efforts at leading his family in worship. The analogy brings to mind visions of lions, tigers, and monkeys running amok, clowns performing all kinds of antics just to make people laugh, and daredevils defying death on tightropes and the flying trapeze. And, that dad wasn't the first one to express to us discouragement over this matter of worship in the home.

Almost every time we've spoken to a group of parents or counseled with parents, this subject seems to come up. We all know that family times dedicated to God are effective and necessary, yet we all can also agree that the moment we try to organize them, everything that can happen will happen. It just seems like that Murphy guy, and his obnoxious law, invade even this reverent part of our family life. And, with time being such a precious commodity, sometimes it hardly seems worthwhile even to make the effort. Everything about today's culture fights every attempt we make at instituting the old reliable family devotions. So if we can't beat the culture, is our only remaining alternative to cave in and let it drive us into the ground?

What if there was a better way? What if, with some minor attitude adjustments and a willingness to change our approach, we could not only achieve significant times with God with our families, but we could actually transform our homes into places where worship happens freely and continually?

In this book, we want to share our experiences and the experiences of other families where worship in the home has worked, in spite of busyness and daily distractions. The ideas are not really new, because God modeled them to His people throughout Scripture. We hope that, as you read this book, the ideas will spark something within you that encourages you and inspires you. We've seen in our family, and in most other families too, that when the home is not a worshipful place, the people who live there are rarely fulfilled in their personal worship before God.

You need to know, at this point, that not everything we ever tried really worked. Some of our efforts to make our home a place of worship actually failed miserably. We've experienced those same "big-top" moments that were so frustrating to that dad who spoke to us. But, this is not a job for quitters. When something fails to make a connection, then try something else. What we've learned through the years is that our efforts don't have to be perfect, but they do have to be purposeful and consistent.

We pray that as you read the pages that follow, you can catch a glimpse of what family worship could look like in your house. Each chapter not only expresses the principles that can make it happen, but you'll also find sidebars full of ideas and activities that will give you some practical direction. These sidebars are an important part of the book and are critical for applying the content of the book to your own family. You can use the suggested activities just as they are offered in the book. Then, after you've gained a little confidence, you can begin to use the creativity that God has placed in you to design worship experiences that are custom-made for your family.

At the end of each chapter, the section "Stone upon Stone" provides a series of questions that will lead you toward a broader understanding of what you've just read. Use these questions to direct your thoughts into a personal application of the chapter's principles and to enlighten you as to how your home can become a place of true worship. Then, allow God's Spirit to have free rein in your life, inspiring you to usher creative relevant worship into your home.

God gives us a clear example of how worship can happen at home in the story of the children of Israel. He introduced His creative intentions to Joshua and the leaders of Israel, and they used them to teach their families about His goodness, His power, and His faithfulness. And though the world has changed drastically, the same principles behind setting up stones in Joshua's day remain practical and effective even in a chaotic culture like ours.

Editor's note on the icons used throughout the book:
An icon precedes each activity suggested by the Singletons in the sidebars. Sometimes activities draw from more than one category. The following icons are found throughout the book:

 Creative Arts: These activities include various crafts, as well as drawing and painting. Creative writing and journaling (online or otherwise) are also included in this category.

 Performing Arts: Generally, these activities involve music, drama, or storytelling; also film and television.

 Physical Activity: These activities require motion and movement, such as walking, mowing the lawn, or playing basketball.

 Service Activity: These activities involve serving and blessing others in the name of Jesus.

 Reading: These activities ask the family to read good books (or other material) together or individually.

 Bible Focus: All of the above activities require thinking about God and His work in the world. However, the heart of these activities is focused interaction with the Word (study, discussion, or memorization) and/or thinking through spiritual issues.

 Prayer Focus: All of the above activities should involve prayer. These activities however focus primarily on prayer, particularly intercession.

Laying the

Foundation

"I will show you what it's like when someone comes to me, listens to my teaching, and then follows it. It is like a person building a house who digs deep and lays the foundation on solid rock. When the floodwaters rise and break against that house, it stands firm because it is well built."
–Luke 6:47–48 (NLT)

*And Joshua set up at Gilgal the twelve stones they had taken out of the Jordan. He said to the Israelites, "In the future when your descendants ask their fathers, 'What do these stones mean?' tell them, 'Israel crossed the Jordan on dry ground.'... He did this so that all the peoples of the earth might know that the hand of the L*ORD *is powerful and so that you might always fear the L*ORD *your God."*
—Joshua 4:20–22,24

Setting Up Stones

Would rocks in your living room draw some attention? Martha creatively illustrates that even in today's culture, out-of-the-ordinary occurrences are certain to catch the attention of the family. Then, Greg recounts the story of Joshua and the children of Israel, when God took care to make an eternal connection with them too.

As Dad's SUV pulls into the driveway at 6:15 on Tuesday evening as expected, the kids glance out to see him opening the back hatch.

Making a trip to the garage, he returns to the back of the truck, pulling his son's old red wagon. Still in his slacks and dress shirt, Dad begins to wrestle his cargo out of the SUV, trying to balance it on the wagon.

As rings of sweat appear on his shirt, he finally manages to precariously wedge a gigantic rock atop the wagon, and begins a slow and careful journey toward the front door, propelling and steering the wagon with one hand, while holding the rock in place with the other.

Jason, 8, watches dumbfounded as Dad rolls the rock off the wagon and onto the porch, and with red-faced determination, shoves it inch by inch across the threshold, down the entry hall, over the carpet and into the center of the family room.

Standing up, Dad wipes his hands on his slacks, stretches his back, grins, and heads upstairs to change clothes.

"What is that, Daddy?" Jason calls after him. Circling the stone several times, Jason begins to see possibilities, and runs to amass his action figure collection for what could be the greatest toy soldier battle of all time.

Fourteen-year-old Jennifer, diet soda in one hand and cell phone pressed to her ear with the other, casts a glance at the rock as she passes through toward the front door. "Was that here before?" she asks Jason.

Coming from the kitchen, Mom pulls up short and glares at the rock. Certain that it's not the new coffee table she's been wanting, she looks at her kids. "Who drug that dirty rock onto my new carpet?" she demands.

"Daddy!" the kids answer in unison, as he comes whistling down the stairs.

Three pairs of eyes fasten on him as Jason voices the question for everyone, "What's that here for?"

Sound far-fetched? Read Joshua 4. This is almost exactly the same scenario that God had in mind for the families of Israel when He gave them instructions before crossing the Jordan River.

Focus on the Goal

Oprah Winfrey says of her great success in the field of entertainment, "The big secret in life is that there is no big secret. Whatever your goal, you can get there if you're willing to work."

Like everything else in life, success is all about work. In order to set up the stones that will make your home a place of worship, tireless effort is required. Sometimes, despite your best efforts, what you were sure would be a can't-miss, surefire way to lead your family into worship will fail miserably. But if you press on, great breakthroughs will happen, as you see your family becoming genuine worshippers.

The goal is to make your home a place that is conducive to authentic worship in a manner that fits your family's style and personality. I'm not certain that you can know what that looks like in your home until you are neck-deep into the process. So, keep trying, keep working, and most importantly, keep worshipping!

Joshua and the children of Israel were in the midst of a whirlwind of changes. Their culture, their way of thinking, their everyday life were about to completely change. For the past 40 years, they had been nomads. Now the land that God had promised Moses was about to become their home.

"Moses my servant is dead" (Joshua 1:2). God's declaration was not a shocking revelation to Joshua. He already knew that Moses, the man he had diligently and faithfully followed, had died. No longer was he to learn at the feet of the man who had discipled him for so many years. Now, it was his turn to lead the people toward God's promise.

In speaking this word to Joshua, God's purpose was to enlighten him to the fact that things weren't going to remain the way they used to be. Soon, they would move into the Promised Land. Joshua, himself, had been one of the spies that Moses had sent in to the land back then, and only he and Caleb had seen past the difficulties and envisioned what could be. But now, as he assumed the responsibility to lead, Joshua realized that the transition might be frightening at times, and the challenges that their new cultural environment presented them were, very often, going to be uncomfortable. Methods were going to have to change. People's way of thinking would be different. Effective communication among tribes and generations was going to require new approaches. But Joshua knew that what God had promised was good. And now, he had to convey his faith and confidence to the Hebrews as they made their journey toward that place of promise.

God gave some distinct marching orders to Joshua, including, "Be strong and courageous" (Joshua 1:6). He told Joshua that he was not to fear what he would inevitably face. God exhorted him that to try to insulate himself from the challenges around him would be folly. He was to fearlessly lead the children of Israel to the place that had been promised them, despite battles, roadblocks, and distractions.

In Joshua 4, the children of Israel faced their first obstacle in entering the land of promise—crossing the Jordan River. Joshua recalled the day that Moses stood before the Red Sea, raised his staff over it, and God miraculously parted the waters for all the people to cross on dry land. A significant happening like that deserved to be talked about. Hebrew parents should have told their children over and over about that occasion, about how God had come through for them. God's power and His faithfulness should have been established in their hearts through that powerful display. But, somehow, that amazing story had faded from their memories in less than a generation!

As the Jordan flowed before them, Joshua called the people together and told them that God had promised, once again, to part the waters and allow them to cross safely to the other side. He told them the story of what he had seen on the shores of the Red Sea as he followed Moses. And, just as God had told him to do, Joshua instructed them as to how the crossing of the Jordan was to take place. God, the Master Teacher, had called His class into session.

Joshua informed the people that God had chosen this moment to teach them about who He is, and to assure them that He is with them always. Their heavenly Father wanted them to know, with certainty, His power and His promises. This act would be a sign to them that He would be faithful to drive out their enemies and deliver them to a new homeland. This was one of those beautiful moments, in which you want to say, "I wish I'd thought of that!" God creatively illustrated that, though everything around them was changing, He is still the same.

But this was a truth that He wanted them to *always* remember. This time, God expected to make such a solid imprint on the people's minds that they would talk about His faithfulness from generation to generation. So, He instructed Joshua that while His hand held the waters back, Joshua should select a man from each tribe to pick up a large stone from the river bottom and bring it to the shore. God required that each man take a stone to his dwelling, where his family was camped, and place it in plain sight.

Just Jump In!

When Greg and I were just starting in youth ministry in the mid-1970s, Wayne Rice and Mike Yaconelli were beginning their reign as the official gurus of youth groups that rock. Although that was not a real organization, all of the youth ministers who attended their seminars wanted to be like them; Rice and Yaconelli were our fearless leaders. We were so impressed that we bought every one of the books in their *Ideas* series, which contained icebreakers, crazy games, and skits for youth groups.

For our first Sunday night back from their conference, we picked out a few activities and headed for the church. But as the kids began to gather, I started to have doubts. What if the kids thought it was stupid? What if it bombed so badly that no one would come back to youth group, because it wasn't cool?

However, when it was time for the first game, I "gutted up," and introduced the activity with as much salesmanship and enthusiasm as I could. And to my amazement, the kids loved it!

We have used those same basic ideas and approaches with both church kids and my high school students for nearly three decades. No matter how cool the kids might pretend to be, they still love it.

So, when it's time to start leading your family to active worship, don't second-guess yourself when it comes to planning activities. It doesn't take much to transform a ho-hum time into one of the best times of the day. Just jump on in there and introduce your ideas with a smile. They'll love it. Really!

Knowing His people as well as He did, God had already anticipated the curiosity that this display was going to stir. He knew what questions were going to be asked.

"In the future your children will ask you, 'What do these stones means?' Then you can tell them, 'They remind us that the Jordan River stopped flowing when the Ark of the Lord's Covenant went across.' These stones will stand as a memorial among the people of Israel forever."
—Joshua 4:6–7 (NLT)

God's idea for using these particular stones was probably a different approach than we would have taken. They weren't to be placed in the city square or the marketplace or even the synagogue. He knew that the best place to make His point was in the home—the place where they were dwelling. He gave those fathers a commission. They were to teach their children true worship of the Almighty God right there in their homes. The task didn't fall to the priests or Hebrew school. The story was to be passed on within the family, from parents to children, from generation to generation. God's intention remains the same today. Our homes are to be the place in which we daily offer Him meaningful worship.

Not only that, but God never intended that learning of His greatness was only to occur within the framework of a tedious and lengthy catechism. Had that been His design, the stones would have been accompanied by scrolls. Instead, He gave them a pattern for creative, exciting, and effective worship that would take place right in their homes. He presented them with an example that was relevant to their culture, and one that

Setting Up Stones

they would never forget. And, in doing so, He created a story about His character that would be passed on to the generations that followed.

Worth the Effort

Making your home a place of worship is not an exact science, in which a combination of formulas guarantees a constant sum. It is instead a creative and ongoing work. Like a piece of music or a sculpture, it requires perspiration as well as inspiration. You have to tirelessly revisit the concept time and time again, refining it, reworking it. Like other works of art, your efforts won't always be successful. With time, though, you'll begin to see some of the rough edges become smoother. Then, your place of worship, like a real work of art, will be unique. The expression of worship in your home will reflect the heart and the personality of your family.

The Smiths had been dutifully trying to have family devotions since Jason could sit up in a highchair without toppling over. But the battle to make it happen has been bloodier than any raid attempted by the most stalwart of Jason's action figures.

Two weeks ago Dad gave it another try. Thinking it would make a great start to the day, Dad opened up his book of 365 devotionals at the breakfast table and began to read. Jennifer propped her elbow on the table to hold her sleepy head and shaded her eyes with her hand. Even Mom kept glancing nervously toward the clock, sensing the bus getting closer and closer to their block, and the lunches hadn't even been packed. Meanwhile, Jason surreptitiously slid the single toy soldier he smuggled to the table dangerously closer to a tiny pool of syrup, collateral damage from the campaign amid the waffles. Everyone jumped guiltily as Dad peered over the cover of the book, pleading for someone to answer question number one.

A few days later, Dad changed the approach, gathering the fam in the living room with 28 minutes to spare before the first show of a new season of "American Idol." People were now wide-awake, there was plenty of time, and Mom smiled encouragingly as Dad reached for the daily devotion he had printed from an email he had received that day. This was definitely going to be better. Two sentences in, the phone rang, and Jennifer's back stiffened, her eyes lit up and she sprang to the edge of the couch, waiting for the signal that she could answer the phone. "Just let it ring," Dad instructed her, and he continued to read. Jennifer slumped back against the couch as the familiar tones of a telemarketer's recorded message drifted from the kitchen. Dad furrowed his brow and inquired of Mom, "Aren't we supposed to be on that no-call list?"

As he continued, the devo was really beginning to build up steam. Elijah was in the cave, and an earthquake was coming. Suddenly, the phone rang once more, sending some sort of shock wave that caused Jennifer's spine to bolt to attention again. This time, it was Lauren's voice leaving Jen an urgent message in her distinctive ninety-words-a-second style. Dad plunged doggedly on, but there was something horribly wrong with Jennifer's face that caused her eyes to roll and her mouth to make little gasping whines. While carpet foraging, Jason had picked up a scrap of paper and was meticulously tearing it up into a neat pile of tiny white squares. Mom had developed a facial condition of her own, one that caused her jaw to tighten, her teeth to clench, her brow to lower, her head to shake violently in short little negative nods, and her eyes to blaze lightning bolts at each kid. It was not a pretty sight.

Having made it all the way through to the last sentence, Dad put down the pages, and like they were fired from a cannon, everyone blasted from the room. Dejectedly, he flipped through the television channels, realizing that he couldn't give it another try anytime soon, because the next day was soccer practice for both kids, Wednesday night was the midweek service at church, and Thursday was the night Jason was supposed to read the story that he wrote at the PTA meeting.

Ideas for Getting Started

Here are a few simple ideas to get you thinking creatively:

Put sheets of art paper, construction paper, or colored typing paper, and a box of crayons or markers in the middle of the table. Ask each family member to draw or write about the aspect of God's character that most attracts them to Him. When everyone has finished, let each person show his or her work and talk about it. Display the papers on the fridge for a while.

Hang a large piece of paper. Go around the family circle and have each person use *one* word to describe God, while the child most able (or a parent) writes the words. You could use dry erase markers to put those words around the edge of the bathroom mirrors, as a reminder for a few days.

(continued)

God had to remind Joshua, *"Be strong and courageous,"* when He commissioned him to build a place of worship. Today's culture is, to say the least, not always conducive to building altars. God didn't instruct Joshua to hunker down when the process was hindered. He called on Joshua to get tough, to persevere, and above all, to not throw up his hands and whine. Setting up stones is not easy work. It requires a keen awareness and diligence. It calls for a plan and a goal. Encouraging your family to become worshippers is not a job for the timid.

Today at the Smith home, Dad is about to completely change the way his family does worship. Desperate to create a sincere hunger for God in the hearts of his kids, he has found something in the story of Joshua and the children of Israel that he believes might really be effective.

With a twinkle in his eye, he asks each person to guess why they think he dragged a rock into the living room.

"You got it for my soldiers, didn't you?!" Jason enthuses.

Thinking to herself that the rock may have fallen out of her husband's head, Mom nevertheless guesses, "Are you going to sand it, and put glass on the top to make a coffee table?"

"I saw them make a pretty cool fountain out of a rock on Trading Spaces once," Jennifer ventures.

"Good ideas," Dad says. "But you're not even close."

"So why is it here, Dad?" Jennifer asks.

"It's here to help us remember, Jen," Dad answers.

"Let me tell you a story," he says. "I'll bet you didn't know that God parted the water for the Israelites two times, did you?"

Mom's mouth drops ever so slightly, and Jason's and Jennifer's eyes are glued on Dad as he tells the story of Joshua, his men, and the stones from the riverbed.

"Now," Dad says, "I brought this stone in because God has done some great things for our family, too, and I want us to remember them, and thank Him."

"Jason, what's the most important thing that God has done for you, buddy?" Dad asks.

Ideas for Getting Started

Play the old parlor game, charades, drawing words that show God's nature, like *father, shepherd, protector, comforter*. Or, use parables, or Old Testament stories, or Bible characters as prompts, too.

Have each family member write the name of their favorite Sunday School song or chorus, and put the slips of paper in a bowl. Each day, draw one out, and sing the song. Talk about what the song means. Do the same thing with favorite Bible verses, or Bible verses about a certain subject you are studying. Work as a group to memorize each verse for that day.

Eyes lighting up, Jason says, "It was when Taffy was sick, and the vet said if the medicine didn't work we might have to put her to sleep, but the medicine did work, and she's still here, because we asked God to make her well."

"What about when Lauren's dad got laid off, and they were going to move to California? You and Mom prayed with me that they would be able to stay, and he got a better job, so Lauren's still my best friend," Jennifer offers.

"I remember when Jen was only three months old, and the doctor thought she had pneumonia, but her fever broke right after we prayed," Mom says.

"I've been watching the Iraqi people on the news every night, and thinking how grateful I am that we go to sleep at night, then wake up in the morning and go about our business, with no fear of what might happen," Dad says.

"Let's just join hands as we stand around this rock, and let it be an altar like those *in Joshua's day, and each say a sentence or two to thank God for being so good to us," he directs. As his family goes around the circle, each expressing simple thanks, Dad smiles. This setting up stones—to create curiosity and involve the whole group in discussion and activity— just may work, he thinks.*

When their prayer ends, Jen gives him a hug. "Thanks, Dad. That was really neat," she says, fishing in her jeans pocket for her cell phone.

"Don't worry, Honey. Jason and I will move the rock as soon as it's light in the morning," Dad assures Mom.

"You know, I really liked that," Mom says. "Why don't we just put the rock in the back flower bed and keep it there as a constant reminder to us?"

When God commissioned the Hebrew fathers to transform their homes into places of worship, He put into place an ongoing system for building believers. God knew His people. He knew that the mere emotion that surrounded a miracle in their midst would not sustain their faith. The spiritual peak that accompanied it wouldn't last. God understood that for people to know Him, they had to think about Him. They had to find His grace and His goodness in the midst of daily happenings. They needed to be reminded over and over again of His love, His might, and His faithfulness. He didn't intend that families simply become passive observers of His presence. God wanted every member of every household to know Him intimately and love Him wholeheartedly.

The stone in the Hebrew family's living room was just as provocative as it would be in yours. God wants us each to make our homes a place of worship, and He wants it to be as exciting and memorable—even in the midst of a PlayStation-and-MTV-culture—as it was on the banks of the River Jordan.

Stone upon Stone

What has been your family's experience when you've tried to establish a regular time of family devotions? Would you consider it to be successful?

What are your family's biggest obstacles when you try to gather for family devotions?

What made setting up stones in the dwelling places such a good idea for the children of Israel?

Does it take more than attending church on Sunday to make a family a worshipping family? What can you work on at home to bring the process along?

What are your spiritual goals for your family?

"But the time is coming—indeed it's here now—when true worshipers will worship the Father in spirit and in truth. The Father is looking for those who will worship him that way."
—John 4:23 (NLT)

2

God's Word on Worship

Greg relates how Grandma's big birthday celebration turned into a sweet time of recalling a simple past. Then, he examines God's perspective on the true meaning of worship. Martha presents some ways that your family can expand their point of view concerning worship.

A few years ago, we all gathered to celebrate Greg's grandmother's 100th birthday. When we asked Grandma how it felt to be 100, she said, "Not a bit different than 99."

Inevitably, she was quizzed about everything she had seen and done during the past century. When she was a little girl, automobiles were such a rarity that everyone had to stop and watch them when they passed by. She never even saw an airplane until she was a teenager, but then, during World War II, she contributed to the war effort by working on them. Even with her technical knowledge of aircraft and how they worked, she still hadn't foreseen air travel to the moon and other planets in her lifetime.

During that birthday celebration, she began to look back at the past, recalling particular scenes from her childhood. Her father was a circuit-riding preacher, a godly man who dispensed fire and brimstone throughout Texas and Oklahoma. He managed to rear nine children who all remained true to the faith that he instilled in them. They faced danger, disease, and the Depression, but throughout the years they were still able to testify of God's unfailing care.

Those times are hardly recognizable in light of our lives now. Grandma's family spent their days picking cotton from one town to the next, from dawn's first light until sunset. All the children helped with the work in the fields, and only occasionally did they attend a one-room schoolhouse. Grandma recalled watching her momma, all four-feet-ten inches and 95 pounds of her, dragging a bag full of cotton that was bigger than she was through the rows. Momma never complained about the backbreaking task, but instead, filled the cotton fields with songs of praise to God. That made an impact on her daughter's life that has lasted almost a century.

As the daily grind of picking cotton came to a close, the girls prepared dinner while the boys put away the cotton bags and tools. Then, following dinner, it was time for family devotions. Every day, except Sunday, which was totally dedicated to being in the house of the Lord, followed the same routine.

The family devotions back then were not anything like we know them today. With no televisions, radios, CD players, video games, Internet, or other entertainment opportunities available, their family worship time became the only focus for the evening. The children, who were deemed indispensable for work in the fields, could not even claim doing homework as a diversion from it.

By the light of kerosene lanterns, the entire evening was filled with singing hymns and reading and memorizing Scripture. One by one, each of the kids dozed off and was carried to bed, until there was nobody left awake to join in. The last sound heard every night was Poppa's strong voice lifted in prayer and song as he doused the lanterns' light.

Grandma, who went to be with the Lord in 2005 at age 102, gave us a beautiful snapshot of a much simpler time. As attractive as the simplicity may seem to some folks today, or, possibly, as unbearable as it may seem to others, it certainly is a scene that would be impossible for most of us to duplicate in today's world. Despite the exhausting work, it seems that it was almost easier for them to find time to worship together way back then. There were no high-tech distractions then, and no requirements of where they had to be and when they had to be there. Their lives and their schedules were much less complex than ours.

Our culture has taken us by the hand and led us on to a merry-go-round that we call life in the twenty-first century. Sometimes it's a lot of fun and very exciting. Other times, people and things seem to pass us by in a blur. It can be uncomfortable. And if we slow down long enough to think about what is happening around us, it may even make us kind of sick.

Though our heads may be left spinning by the mad whirl we call life, there still is one truth that we can reach for and hold on to. God never changes. His power, creativity, and love are the same today as when Grandma was a little girl in the cotton fields, as well as when He spoke the universe into existence. The same Truth that her preacher poppa proclaimed in brush arbors from town to town is alive and well today.

In the lives of men and women chronicled in the Bible and in the lives of saints through history, God has proven to us over and over again that He is creative and personal. His nature and His character are constant, but He speaks a unique language that connects with each human being throughout time and across the globe.

God told Joshua to remove stones from the very place that the Hebrews had crossed a river on dry land, just so He could connect with His people. God gave David psalms, and, in songwriters throughout history, He inspired hymns and choruses, just so He could connect with His people. Jesus told stories about fishing to fishermen and about planting to farmers, just so He could connect with His people.

Today, God is not asking us to drag our family, kicking and screaming, back to some bygone era where they can know Him and learn of His ways. He wants us to partner with Him to use the good, the bad, and the ugly of the twenty-first century to show our family that He is just as relevant, just as powerful, and just as loving today as He has been at any time in the history of civilization.

Without selling out or giving in, how can we utilize today's culture to make our family worship alive? Perhaps the place to begin is to redefine some of the things we do that we call worship and to reexamine how we do them.

In Spirit and Truth

Jesus addressed this very issue when He rested at the well with the Samaritan woman one day (John 4). His insight had demonstrated to her that He was a man with a distinctive perspective. Perhaps the subject of worship had been a hot topic of conversation around town, or maybe, simply, her spiritual condition had produced within her a longing for more of God. It was on her mind, and she was seeking insightful wisdom that day. The question on her mind, the dilemma, was concerning where worship was supposed to happen. The Jews taught that the temple in Jerusalem was the only place where true worship took place. The Samaritan woman's culture had taught her that the place of real worship was on Mount Gerizim.

Jesus's reply, as was often the case, brought a fresh viewpoint to the mix. He told her that the focus of worship was not to be on habitual ceremonies and traditions of the culture. Nor was the emphasis to be on a place or a posture.

> *"But the hour is coming, and now is," He said, "when the true worshipers will worship the Father in spirit and truth; for the Father is seeking such to worship Him."*
> —John 4:23 (NKJV)

Jesus's words made all the cultural conflicts seem trivial and inconsequential. His straightforward statement was full of clarity. True worship, He said, is an authentic expression of adoration and praise for who God is and what He's done.

In His conversation with the woman, Jesus gave simple but eternal insight into God's characterization of true worship. This concept offers us three key truths that enable us to make our homes a place of worship. True worship is a lifestyle, it is wholehearted, and it is honest.

True worship is a lifestyle. The Samaritan woman tried to frame worship in the context of her culture. Jesus's reply frees us to worship independently of any constraint of time, place, or rituals.

In Romans 12:1, Paul urges believers to offer their entire beings, their whole lives, as living sacrifices before God.

> So here's what I want you to do, God helping you: Take your everyday, ordinary life—your sleeping, eating, going-to-work, and walking-around life—and place it before God as an offering. Embracing what God does for you is the best thing you can do for him.
> —Romans 12:1 (*The Message*)

Our worship need not be confined to a cathedral, or a designated period of time that is accompanied by skillful musicians. What we do on Sundays at church is merely a corporate expression of the worship that we have lived throughout the week. To limit worship to those Sunday expressions ignores the creative nature that God invests within each one of us. God gave us the gift of artistic resourcefulness so that we could lavish praise upon Him. He didn't intend for our offerings of worship to all look alike. The setting does not dictate the worship, but, instead, the true worshipper decides how he or she will present the offering of praise. What would happen if we would begin to view our entire lives as unique expressions of worship? What if our worship wasn't isolated to a few moments during our day, but was found in every task, every interaction, and every moment we lived. Just imagine how our actions, communication, and attitudes would drastically change!

It all starts with the simple things. The most important step that we as families can make to set up stones is to be consistent in our lifestyles. Please note that perfection is not what's required of us. But, in the way we live our lives every day, in the way we communicate in our home, it's crucial that our goal be to reflect God's character. Our focus should be to love our kids the way God loves, discipline them the way He disciplines, and teach them the way He teaches. We need to become intentional about loving our spouse and partnering together the way God does with each of us. We, individually, have to be totally committed to this process. And along the way, we can be sure that our families will readily see a truer picture of us as we seek to live a life of worship in spirit and truth.

God compels us to adopt this lifestyle of worship, and our response reveals to Him, and those who are close to us, the authenticity of our heart. That can't happen if we compartmentalize our lives, offering only a part of ourselves, or a part of our time, to worshipping Him. When we've dedicated ourselves to a personal lifestyle of true worship, we will begin to reflect the beauty of God at work in us.

True worship is wholehearted. Vince Lombardi was an amazing man. The former coach of the National Football League's Green Bay Packers embraced a philosophy of living that not only produced winning football teams but has served as motivation for countless other success stories in other venues. Above all else, Coach Lombardi preached wholehearted commitment. He said, "Unless a man believes in himself and makes a total commitment to his career, and puts everything he has into it—his mind, his body, his heart—what's life worth to him?"

A worship lifestyle requires that same type of commitment. In Matthew 23, the religious leaders sought to trap Jesus when they asked Him, "Which is the greatest commandment in the Law?" (Matthew 22:36). But Jesus would not allow Himself to be drawn into a theological argument. His answer was not beyond debate: "'Love the Lord your God with all your heart and with all your soul and with all your mind.' This is the first and greatest commandment" (v. 37–38). God's plan for His people is wrapped up in that single statement. When Jesus spoke that irrefutable truth before the religious leaders, their arguments were defenseless. Wholehearted devotion to God both transcends and fulfills any other efforts or considerations.

The Samaritan woman, like many of the religious people of the day, also was seeking a debate. Because she perceived Jesus to be a knowledgeable and godly man, she began to frame an intellectual discussion about worship. Jesus's response revealed to her that worship can't be comprehended by exhausting the facts concerning the subject. Worshipping *"in spirit and truth"* implies much more depth than a cursory acknowledgement of God, and much more breadth than intense mental calisthenics. Our heavenly Father responds to our wholehearted expressions of devotion. That, alone, is the foundation of worship and intimacy with Almighty God.

More Than Just Good Manners

Your mom was right—always say *please* and *thank you*. Whether she realized it or not, these seemingly mundane expressions have far more impact than ensuring socially acceptable behavior. Developing a thankful heart, or, conversely, an attitude of ungratefulness, is a habit. So, fill your home with thankfulness!

It starts with Mom and Dad—saying *please*, *thank you*, and *you're welcome*. Then declare it to be a family trait—"Our family expresses thanks!" Expressions of thankfulness are like the reins and the bridle in the horse's mouth. They will turn the tide of attitude in your home.

The Bible tells us, "So then, just as you received Christ Jesus as Lord, continue to live in him, rooted and built up in him, strengthened in the faith as you were taught, and overflowing with thankfulness" (Colossians 2:6–7).

John and Charles Wesley changed the world. The brothers were unrelenting in their dedication to serving God and were at the forefront of one of history's greatest spiritual renewals. Like Lombardi dedicated himself to his sport, the Wesleys' devotion to God was focused and uncompromising. John once encouraged believers to "sing *lustily*, and with good courage. Beware of singing as if you were half dead, or half asleep, but lift up your voice with strength" (*The Revised Compendium of Methodism*, James Porter, 1875, http://books.google.com)

Charles penned the lyrics to "Soldiers of Christ, Arise!" in 1749 as a challenge for the church to dedicate itself to serving God without reservation.

Soldiers of Christ, arise, and put your armor on,
Strong in the strength which God supplies through His eternal Son.
Strong in the Lord of hosts, and in His mighty power,
Who in the strength of Jesus trusts is more than conqueror.

Stand then in His great might, with all His strength endued,
But take, to arm you for the fight, the panoply of God;
That having all things done, and all your conflicts passed,
Ye may o'ercome through Christ alone and stand entire at last.

From strength to strength go on, wrestle and fight and pray,
Tread all the powers of darkness down and win the well fought day.
Still let the Spirit cry in all His soldiers, "Come!"
Till Christ the Lord descends from high and takes the conquerors home.

(See Ephesians 6:13–18.)

True worship is honest. God is seeking pure hearts, right attitudes, and real honesty. Authenticity is vital to fresh, real worship. Becoming authentic entails coming before Almighty God just as we are. That takes courage and faith. It requires an understanding that this is the way God accepts us, unreservedly. He doesn't hold us at arm's length until we can first get it all together. Thank God for that. It's our honesty before Him that is attractive to Him. The heart of God is revealed in Psalm 51:17: "I learned God-worship when my pride was shattered. Heart-shattered lives ready for love don't for a moment escape God's notice" (*The Message*).

As a parent, nothing breaks down walls more decidedly than when your child comes to you and says, "I've messed up. I'm so sorry. But I want you to hug me. I need you to still love me." There's no need for anything else to be discussed at that point. When we approach God with the same authenticity, He doesn't hesitate to accept us. He is moved.

Part of honesty in worship is gratitude in worship. A heart of true worship is based on an attitude of gratitude. Noted author and Bible teacher Charles Swindoll writes:

> The longer I live, the more I realize the impact of attitude on life. I am convinced that life is 10 percent what happens to me and 90 percent how I react to it.... This may shock you, but I believe the single most significant decision I can make on a day-to-day basis is my choice of attitude. It is more important than my past, my education, my bankroll, my successes or failures, fame or pain, what other people think of me or say about me, my circumstances, or my position.
> —Charles Swindoll, *Man to Man*

That's the reason an attitude of thankfulness is so important in true worship. Approaching God with anything less than heartfelt thankfulness belies the very truth upon which our relationship with Him is built. A thankless heart denies the magnitude of Jesus's sacrifice. It rejects the daily blessings that God heaps upon us. It is dishonest about the reality of God's love for us and His acceptance of us. The Bible calls us to be thankful in all circumstances (see 1 Thessalonians 5:18). So thankfulness can't be dependent on our situation. It is, instead, a choice that we make.

A grateful heart can't be developed overnight. It requires a readjustment of our viewpoint. Its foundation is built upon a daily decision to be a person of thankfulness. The true worshipper, through willing repetition, builds an attitude of gratefulness that gives his or her worship authenticity. To simply say it's a habit that we develop, though, trivializes the spiritual healing that being thankful actually accomplishes in our lives. Once we begin to verbalize gratefulness, even when we may not feel it, we soon discover that we actually *become* grateful. And that opens the floodgates for true overflowing worship in us and in our families.

Free to Worship

What will it look like when your home is a place of worship? That will be different in each and every family. The personalities under each roof determine what form the worship takes on. Authentic worship, however, will be creative. Just as Jesus taught the woman at the well, real worship in your home won't necessarily be like some other family's expressions. True worshipping parents will express their worship genuinely and wholeheartedly in all that they do. They will encourage heartfelt expressions from every member of the household.

We have to avoid the temptation to make the family worship look the way *we* want it to look. One of the most significant aspects of developing a worshipful home is to allow your children to be free in their worship. In church, the Scripture requires that there be order, because it's a corporate gathering. Worship there, where a larger group is involved, is necessarily guided and controlled. Home, though, should be more like a worship workshop. It needs to be the place where each individual can freely express himself or herself to God. The free exercise of worship allows us to build a comfort level in our relationship with God.

By the time your kids reach their teens, peer pressure usually does a great job of pushing them into an unwritten code of self-restraint. There will be times when you will have to subdue the urge within you to try to make them more expressive in relating to God. But the younger ones usually are a bundle of uninhibited creativity. Often, things that they say or do in their response to God may not exactly fit your experience of worship, or may be less than acceptable from an adult frame of reference. And that's OK.

I recall a few times when I heard my small children articulate and model their true worship and, I'm sad to say, it almost embarrassed me. I reasoned that it wasn't the way I would do it, or it might not be accepted if some of our church people heard it. Thankfully, through the years, I realized that I was the one who needed to mature! I recalled Jesus's impassioned command, "Let the little children come to me" (Matthew 19:14). I learned that my responsibility was not as much to teach them how to worship, but to introduce them to a God who deserved wholehearted praise. They not only needed to see and hear me worship, they needed to know what I felt about God. I learned from them what a

How Many Ways to Worship?

Try brainstorming with your family about every way you can think of to worship God. Almost any age group can participate in this exercise, and it will expand your family's concept of worship. This can be a project that stretches over an extended period of time, because, in reality, there are limitless responses to this. Feel free to allow your kids to use their imaginations. Search for the different ways that people in the Bible worshipped God.

The Book of Psalms is the perfect source to teach your children what worship looks like and sounds like. With your family gathered together, search through the entire book to find all the different ways to worship that are mentioned. The list is almost inexhaustible, and offers such a variety of postures and practices that anyone can find something that's a comfortable expression for them—be still, sing, shout, clap your hands, stand, sit, lie down, leap, and on and on. For school-age children, you can achieve greater impact by writing all the responses on butcher paper or poster board.

joyful worshipping heart really looks like. In the midst of our teaching them about true worship, may we never squelch our kids' genuine expression of worship to their heavenly Father!

God gave a foundation on which to build your place of worship in Colossians. He painted a vibrant picture of what the worshipping family looks like.

> *Let the Word of Christ—the Message—have the run of the house. Give it plenty of room in your lives. Instruct and direct one another using good common sense. And sing, sing your hearts out to God! Let every detail in your lives—words, actions, whatever—be done in the name of the Master, Jesus, thanking God the Father every step of the way.*
> —Colossians 3:16–17 (*The Message*)

I don't know about you, but I don't want a quiet house. I want my family to know that real worship can't be confined to the church sanctuary. I want to hear joy and laughter and singing. In fact, I want my family to hear *my* joy and *my* laughter and *my* singing! Just like Poppa used to preach from town to town, "You better get used to it, because it sure ain't gonna be quiet in heaven!"

Stone upon Stone

Jesus said to the woman at the well, *"True worshipers will worship the Father in spirit and truth"* (John 4:23 NKJV). What does that mean to you?

Has your view of worship hindered or helped how God might want to work in your family? In what ways?

How might you have limited God because of preconceived ideas of *where* worship can take place?

Is there any part of your life that you haven't been willing to offer as worship to God? Are there other inconsistencies in your life that hinder your home from becoming a place of worship? (Romans 12:1; Hebrews 12:1)

Setting Up Stones

The Lord appeared to us in the past, saying: "I have loved you with an everlasting love; I have drawn you with loving-kindness."
—Jeremiah 31:3

3

Called into Relationship

Greg tells about his baseball hero, then Martha shares some excellent ideas on how to teach your family about the greatness of our God.

From the time I first became interested in baseball until I was almost grown, my favorite player was Baltimore Orioles third baseman Brooks Robinson. Every day, I'd search the box scores to see how he'd done in the game the night before. I celebrated with him when he had a great day, and I suffered with him when he went zero for four. I knew his history, I knew his stats, and I watched every move he made on the baseball field. I wanted to hit like him, field like him, throw like him, and run like him.

With apologies to Mr. Robinson, although he was a very good baseball player—a Hall of Famer, in fact—he wasn't the best player of that era. I didn't admire him and emulate him because he was incomparable; there was another reason that I was his biggest fan.

One spring day when I was just barely in grade school, my Dad took me to a preseason major league baseball game *in my hometown!* That was a real treat for a little boy in San Antonio, Texas, because the closest big-league baseball at the time was played in St. Louis. I entered old Mission Stadium in awe. My baseball cards had come to life! Before the game started, I made my way down to the dugout area to be as close to the ballplayers as possible. And, there, I came face-to-face with Brooks Robinson. He looked me in the eye and smiled, took my pen, and autographed my souvenir program. He said something to me, but everything was such a blur that I don't recall exactly what it was. From that moment on, though, Brooks Robinson was my baseball hero. As a result of that brief meeting, I felt like I knew him. In my little-boy mind, he was my friend.

From that moment on, I devoured everything there was to know about Brooks Robinson. I learned from the back of his baseball card that he was from Arkansas and that his nickname was "The Human Vacuum Cleaner," because he was such a great fielder. He was the American League Most Valuable Player in 1964, and his batting average that year was .317! Even though he never gave another thought about that little boy with the pen in San Antonio, I knew everything there was to know about Brooks Robinson. He was my hero. Even today, when I think about him, I wish I could still watch him play third base on the Saturday game of the week on TV. I still have his autograph packed away in a box of my childhood mementos.

Friends with Our Maker?

Isn't it amazing how an encounter with the famous or nearly famous can affect our lives? The connection, however brief, and usually never to be repeated, can set in motion a lifelong feeling of association. Suppose, however, that the person of renown actually wanted to know *you* better. What if they desired to build a relationship with you and become your best friend?

When we reach the full realization that Almighty God, the Creator of the Universe, made the ultimate effort to reach out to us, it is, without a doubt, life changing. This is the foundational truth of worship. What a thought! He desires, above all else, to have a relationship, an intimate friendship, with you and me. God created us to have fellowship with Him. We were made to worship Him, love Him, embrace Him.

There is a problem, though. The sin of Adam and Eve, passed on through each succeeding generation, has given us each of us a sinful nature, producing a chasm that prevents human beings from enjoying a relationship with God in the way He intended. Because of that isolation, we experience the frustration, hurt, and emptiness of a life estranged from God. Without His gift of salvation, we cannot enjoy friendship with God. We can't come close to Him to speak to Him. His presence is hidden from us, so we can't see Him clearly. From that, we experience fear and uncertainty about our past, present, and future.

God can't fellowship where sin exists because He is completely holy. Because He is perfect, imperfection not only blocks any relationship with Him, it cannot even share space with Him. To think anything else is possible belies the very nature and character of God. There is no good-enough-to-get-by as far as God's holiness is concerned.

But, in our flesh, we still think that if we really can make ourselves good enough, maybe God will receive us. The fact is, though, our feeble attempts at being good and righteous are literally nothing compared to the holiness of God. Isaiah says, "all our righteous acts are like filthy rags" (Isaiah 64:6). The One who created us is the absolute essence of all holiness, all power, all wisdom, and all love. He, alone, is worthy of worship, but our sinful condition prevents our participation. In Isaiah 46:3–9, God Himself defined His credentials for His rebellious creation.

> *"To whom will you compare me? Who is my equal? Some people pour out their silver and gold and hire a craftsman to make a god from it. Then they bow down and worship it! They carry it around on their shoulders, and when they set it down, it stays there. It cannot even move! And when someone prays to it, there is no answer. It can't rescue anyone from trouble. Do not forget this! Keep it in mind! Remember this, you guilty ones. Remember the things I have done in the past. For I alone am God! I am God, and there is none like me."*
> —Isaiah 46:3–9 (NLT)

If our guilt were the final word, life would be hopeless. There would never be any way to make the relationship right again. The lack of fulfillment in our lives would eat away at us, bringing frustration and emptiness.

But, thank God, there's more.

My favorite story in all the Scriptures is a picture that is painted at the death of Jesus on the Cross. As the Son of God laid down His life on the Cross, breathing His final labored breath, He uttered, "It is finished!" (John 19:30 NLT). It was a declaration of completion rather than an admission of defeat. Jesus, like an innocent lamb, took on Himself all the sin that we had committed. "For God made Christ, who never sinned, to be the offering for our sin, so that we could be made right with God through Christ" (2 Corinthians 5:21 NLT).

What followed was one of the most graphic demonstrations of God's love, and I'm always moved when I think about it. As Jesus breathed His last on the Cross, the heavy drape in the temple, which separated the Holy of Holies from the rest of the temple, was ripped from top to bottom. What an amazing symbol God used to speak to us! The price of our sin, which separated us from Him, had been paid with the blood of His own Son, allowing for relationship to be restored.

Up until that time, the Holy of Holies was hidden away behind that drape, symbolizing the separation of God's presence from the people. Only the high priest could enter there, and only once a year, bringing the petitions and offerings of the people before Almighty God. And, by no means was his entry a casual event. Ritualistic cleansing, prayers, supplications and sacrifices, and elaborate preparations preceded the priest's entry. And, still, so uncertain was his acceptance into that holy place that the people attached bells to the hem of his robe as a signal. If the priest's unworthiness caused him to be struck dead in the Holy of Holies, then the sound of the bells would cease. In order to retrieve his lifeless body from the holy place, a rope was to be tied on to his ankle prior to his entry.

Drawing Near

We become intimately acquainted with God through Scripture, which reveals wonderful details about our heavenly Father.

Discover these details about God as a family by reading a brief portion from Psalms, Proverbs, or the Gospels each day for a while. Make a list of facts about God as you proceed, such as: *He knows the number of hairs on our heads*; *He calls us by name*; *He will never leave us;*, *He never sleeps*; *He spoke creation into being*; and others.

Write these truths about God on small squares of colored paper, and glue them to magnets, to decorate the refrigerator. Or, attach them to a coat hanger with colorful yarn, to make a mobile. Decorate and embellish to whatever extent the fam is up for, as we say in our house.

If your family is more the rough-and-tumble type, then use sidewalk chalk, and write facts about God in squares you mark off on the driveway. Depending on the age and ability of your kids, set it up as hopscotch, and say the phrases as you hop to each square. Or set up a pattern around the basketball hoop, and say each one as you shoot your way through the pattern.

What a difference a day makes! When Jesus completed His mission on the Cross, God not only made a way for us to fellowship with Him, He tore down the very symbol of separation. That was His dynamic invitation to us! There was no way that He could say it more emphatically or make it any clearer. By the blood of His Son Jesus Christ, God, our Father, restored the potential for His relationship with us again.

The most amazing part of the story is that we not only have the privilege of being in His presence again, we can be adopted into the very family of Almighty God. When we accept His plan of redemption, He makes a way for us not only to approach Him, but to enjoy the very closest of relationships. He calls us His children. By the blood of Jesus Christ shed on the Cross and His glorious resurrection, we are adopted into God's family. And all the blessings and privileges of that adoption become ours. What a story!

It's About Him

The wonderful story of the gospel is not at all about what we can do to earn acceptance. The focus is completely on what God did and does and how He has made a way for us to have a relationship with Him. The very heart of our worship is the acknowledgement of God's awesome greatness. British songwriter Matt Redman's "Heart of Worship" contains a message that has called the church's attention back to what should have already been obvious to us. This song has been sung around the world, across denominational lines, as an anthem of both repentance and determination. Its sincerity and honesty express the hearts of believers who are longing to experience, once again, the intimacy of fellowship with God. The song expresses that the foundation of worship does not rest in the quality of the music that accompanies it, or in any emotion that can be stirred up in response to how we feel at the moment. Worship is all about Jesus.

In an effort to perhaps be more sophisticated, we often let the obvious slip right through our fingers. Knowing who God is and enjoying His presence have little to do with defining Him. He's not a laboratory experiment or a series of historical facts and events that we can so confidently analyze and discuss. What we must know about God is that He is far bigger than what we can define, express, or even comprehend.

That is the essence of worship. God, who exceeds anything we can imagine, simply wants to have fellowship with us. We don't have to figure it all out, reaching a level of sophistication or intellect to make it work. A person can know a lot about God and the Bible without knowing the God of the Bible. He wants us to know Him personally. What He desires for us is far beyond just an acknowledgment of His existence, it is a closeness that we can enjoy only through experiencing a deep relationship with Him.

That is exactly why we were created—to enjoy a real friendship with our Creator. For that reason, God has been intimately involved in our lives before we even considered Him.

> *You know me inside and out,*
> *you know every bone in my body;*
> *You know exactly how I was made, bit by bit,*
> *how I was sculpted from nothing into something.*
> *Like an open book, you watched me grow from conception to birth;*
> *all the stages of my life were spread out before you,*
> *The days of my life all prepared*
> *before I'd even lived one day.*
> —Psalm 139:15–16 (*The Message*)

As He created us, He anticipated the joy of being our friend, and of being our God. He made us each a unique package, different from all His other creations. He looks forward to a daily expression of worship from you and from me, expressions that are different from everyone else's. There is only one logical response on our part.

> *I thank you, High God—you're breathtaking!*
> *Body and soul, I am marvelously made!*
> *I worship in adoration—what a creation!*
> —Psalm 139:14 (*The Message*)

If, indeed, we were created to worship, invited to worship, then our priority must be to know God more intimately. Worship finds its vitality through experience. Worshipping God, without knowing Him, is like trying to describe the pleasure of eating chocolate cake without ever having tasted one. Knowing who God is and experiencing a more intimate relationship with Him is a process. The recipe is not difficult, but there are no shortcuts to getting the desired results. The Book of James says, "Draw near to God and He will draw near to you" (James 4:8 NKJV).

Leading our families to become true worshippers requires that we are personally and individually experiencing the joy and reality of vital fellowship with God. We have to understand that we are a part of God's story. And in His story He wants to make us complete in Him, enjoying Him forever. God gave His all so that we could experience that type of intimacy with Him .

God intends for each of us to grasp the enormity of helpless humanity's redemption, how we've been cleansed and given purpose by a holy and mighty God. He wants us to know who He is, who we are, and what He has, through grace, made us to be. In order for us to become true worshippers, we must seek Him, we must know Him, we must love Him, and we must experience Him.

Stone upon Stone

What keeps you from having fellowship with God? Are you trying to make yourself clean enough to enter into His presence? Is that going to work? Why or why not? (Isaiah 64:6; Colossians 2:11–15)

How does a person obtain access into God's presence? (1 Peter 3:18; Romans 5; Ephesians 3:12)

Who does God say you are? What does He think of you? (Psalm 139; John 15:15; Galatians 4:1–7)

In your family, when you talk about God, is your purpose to know Him, or just to know about Him? How would those two discussions look different?

God, investigate my life; get all the facts firsthand.
I'm an open book to you;
even from a distance, you know what I'm thinking.
You know when I leave and when I get back;
I'm never out of your sight.
You know everything I'm going to say
before I start the first sentence.
I look behind me and you're there,
then up ahead and you're there, too—
your reassuring presence, coming and going.
This is too much, too wonderful—
I can't take it all in!
—Psalm 139:1–6 (*The Message*)

4

I Gotta Be Me

Questions, questions, questions! There were times when Greg just got tired of them. Here he presents some simple and important guidelines for handling questions that every parent needs to know. Martha then offers some ideas on authentic communication in your family, paving the way for real worship.

I still recall those days early each semester when I scoured the shelves of the university bookstore to select the required textbooks for my courses. Used textbooks were a particularly valuable find. Not only were they less expensive, but a well-worn one could contain a treasure of notes that some brilliant student had attentively chronicled in the margins. It was as if I were searching for some secret code or the key to unlocking a wealth of knowledge and success. And the horror of it, if I discovered, weeks into the course, that these notes weren't the musings of a brilliant scholar but were, in fact, nothing more than the inane scribblings of another struggling learner. Sometimes just obtaining the right used books was as challenging as the course itself!

I'm now convinced that first-time parents should be given a required list of textbooks. The parental reading list should start with a detailed study Bible, alongside another version that puts the text on a level that any child can comprehend. A great set of encyclopedias is a must. And, how about some good bedtime reading to share with the kids? Something like a palatable fantasy that would comfort and calm rather than provoke edginess and nightmares would be valuable. Of course, they should shop used bookstores for all those classic titles that address every childhood challenge they'll face—discipline issues, illnesses, and all the other subjects worth covering. And they'll need to be sure to look for the ones with really good notes in the margins. Won't they wish they knew how the previous owners' kids turned out?

Our daughter Anne started talking early. And, once she opened her mouth, she began a barrage of questions that strung on until she reached her teens. "Daddy, why do horses have four legs?" "Hey, Mom! Do you know why the sky is blue?" "Why does the car make noise when it goes?" "Is Texas the best state to live in?" At times it seemed like an endless stream. She needed answers and she needed them *now!*

I tried to answer each and every query to the best of my abilities, but sometimes she simply wore me down. "Annie, I don't know why. I don't know everything." That was definitely the wrong response. That statement frustrated her. In her little mind, if I didn't have all the answers, I didn't have any of them at all.

"Well, then you don't even know me!" she would reply. That became her staple comeback. When I was exasperated by her questions, she would fire it back at me.

Despite her challenge, I knew one thing for certain. It would be foolish of me to just make up answers. She was seeking truth and reality, and even at her young age, I couldn't afford to be a phony. If she discovered that Daddy had been bluffing about some of the facts, as insignificant as they may have seemed, how could she be sure I was telling the truth when it concerned the important things in life?

Genuine Family, Authentic Faith

Knowing God is the foundation of worship. And the first impressions of God that our children receive are from what Mom and Dad tell them about Him. It's not simply what we verbalize, our actions also prompt them as to how they should perceive their heavenly Father. As cautious as we might be in trying to say all the right things, our authenticity and honesty speak volumes about what our relationship to God is and how real it is for us.

All worship starts with being real. Worship in the home starts with being real in your finest hours and at your worst, in the midst of pressure and on the mountaintop of victory. How we act or react in the midst of all those day-to-day happenings speaks loudest to our children about what a relationship with God looks like. Our children are imitators, and, I don't know about you, but that has always scared me to death. There is nothing that is more convicting than when you see the questionable attitudes and actions you displayed being modeled by your kids.

The children of Israel faced incredible challenges, and at the same time, partook of divine provisions. They endured frustrating disappointments and witnessed miraculous intervention. Their journey wasn't easy, but it was definitely exciting. Have you ever played "If I were God"? I read about some of the antics that the Hebrews pulled and, if I had been God, I would have shut them down in a hurry. I think a crisp but firm thump on the head would have been appropriate. Thankfully, God isn't like me. Through grace and mercy, He still entrusted to them the responsibility of passing on His story.

That responsibility continues today for believing parents. Despite our failings and weaknesses, God has chosen us and commissioned us. We often discuss our charge to reach out to the world, and that's certainly a valid calling on all our lives, but I think we don't consider often enough our mission inside our own homes. Perhaps it's because our obligation to our children seems a bit more daunting and complicated. The pressure can be intense. It's intimidating to think that the potential for failure stares us in the face every day and is on display for the whole world to see. We tend to avoid things that we can't easily manage.

For me, as a dad, there seemed to be so much detail to parenting that it was almost scary. Part of it may have been that our first was a little girl, and I had never been around little girls much. Whatever the reason, I perceived that there was this narrow margin of error in rearing a child, kind of like walking a tightrope.

But in our desire to get it exactly right, we may miss the obvious. As my kids grew up, I realized that God has even more concern for them than I do. I began to find relief and healing in that fact.

There's not a surefire method that guarantees success in making our home a place of worship. One certainty, though, is that if we demonstrate our own real, practical relationship with God in good times and bad, our children are more likely to find that kind of lifestyle attractive. That kind of authenticity teaches them that when the inevitable challenges confront us, there is a place where they can find help and strength. We don't have to protect them from our own honest struggles if we truly are seeking God. When they see the vitality of our relationship with the Lord—that it can stand the stress and strain—the practicality of it draws them. There have been occasional quirky trends throughout history, where the fakes and phonies were regarded as some kind of heroes. But, for the most part, being genuine has always been most valued. More today than ever before, people are drawn to those who can be real.

What does that kind of honesty look like in our families? Simply answering questions is a good place to start.

"Why, Daddy?"

"Because I'm the Daddy and I say so!"

I confess. I've been guilty of it, and so were my parents, and their parents probably were too. Before I had children, I promised myself that I wouldn't be *that* kind of parent. But, for all my fervent pledges, I caught myself, early in the game, giving in to the frustration and pulling rank on my kids.

Do the kids really deserve an answer when we lay down the law? Officially, no. Simply because, as the parents, we *are* the authority. But there is an honesty, a gracefulness, as we gently explain our decisions and our discipline. We don't relinquish anything when we choose to communicate. At one point during my parenting, I think I must have held the notion that the louder I could say, "NO!" the more strength I could demonstrate and the more respect I could command. Thankfully, there came a time when I discovered that communication with my kids, seasoned with steadfastness and consistency, is much more effective, and tends to prevent any long-term accumulation of resentment. I decided that is was much healthier if their faces showed comprehension rather than a crushed spirit.

As in any parent-child interaction, of course, when we respond to their questions we need to do so in age-specific ways. At age nine, my son Matt began to ask me about how babies were made. It wasn't a passing, surface interest that I detected. He wanted some serious answers, approaching the subject with more honesty than we ever had before. I decided it was time for that father-to-son talk that dads dread. I wanted to face it head-on and do it the right way. I decided I'd face it like I used to take medicine when I was a kid—close my eyes, hold my nose, take care of business, and it would be over before I knew it.

Thank God for Larry. He was the owner of the Christian bookstore where I had shopped for years, and he had sons of his own. I told him the situation I was facing, and he assured me that he had a video that would take care of the whole thing. So I purchased it, along with the accompanying study guide. I was ready for anything. I found a cabin in the country that would provide the appropriate backdrop for a focused, deep discussion of the facts of life. If any dad had ever been prepared for this, it was me.

We checked into the cabin and settled in for this momentous occasion. I took a deep breath, and popped the video into the VCR. The TV screen flickered with animated figures that detailed specifically for a nine-year-old what made a man a man and a woman a woman. I watched Matt out of the corner of my eye. He

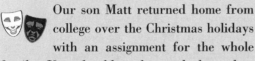

Rescue Stories

Our son Matt returned home from college over the Christmas holidays with an assignment for the whole family. You should understand that when three out of the four people in your family have degrees in education, this is not an unusual occurrence. The task he gave each of us was to present our "rescue story" to the rest of the family during the holidays. He described rescue stories as our personal narratives about the occasions when God intervened in a big way in each our lives. It could be the time when we accepted Christ's salvation, but didn't have to be. But it had to be a place and time that we knew God was real and personal in our lives. Our family's times of sharing during that Christmas were meaningful and memorable. There was plenty of laughter and tears, and we felt a closeness to each other and to our ever-present God. The great thing about these stories is that there are at least dozens of them in each person's life, and the number increases as each day passes, so it can be more than a one-time exercise. It's a great opportunity to reveal to your family the real you and the real God who is with you!

squinted, then flinched. His eyes grew big and his mouth dropped open. He was definitely taking it all in, and I was proud of myself for creating this moment.

At the conclusion of the video, the study guide directed me to encourage discussion. And I wasn't exactly sure how to start.

It was uncomfortably quiet in that cabin, and I figured I was obligated to break the iciness of the moment.

"So what do you think?"

"Yuck!"

"Yuck!?" That was it? No questions to springboard from? No comments that demanded follow-up? That was the extent of Matt's observations. In all my preparations for the moment, I wasn't quite ready for this. My nine-year-old didn't need the depth of honesty that I could provide. He wasn't asking for the specific biology. I found out that the information he was requiring was more on a surface level.

I learned then that while it was never right to misinform kids, authentic interaction should be gauged by the age factor. I wasn't about to humor Matt with stories of the stork or cabbage patches. I wanted to be real, and that weekend taught me how that needed to happen. Presenting reality to your children calls for total honesty, but it requires honesty in doses. Share a little truth, then listen. Answer questions, then determine if there are still more questions. It's the simple secret of communication that we learn to use in business and in interaction with adults. I had to learn that it works with my kids too. It's a pattern that is effective whether you're discussing with them the facts of life, family financial matters, global terrorism, or the greatness of God.

Fear blocks that free flow of authenticity. Almost everyone has a fear of vulnerability— that sinking feeling that, somehow, if we show we're less than perfect, then disastrous consequences will assuredly follow. *What if I'm not accepted any longer? Will they think less of me? Will I relinquish some kind of control?* As we grow in honest communication within our family, those questions and fears begin to crumble.

Being genuine creates an atmosphere at home that cultivates many of the attitudes a Christian family should find very attractive. It breaks down walls that block communication. By creating the awareness that everyone has strengths and weaknesses, it encourages teamwork. And, it lays a foundation of honesty, which affects each family member's relationship with each other and with God.

Words to Live By

For those who find it difficult to be genuine, there is a starting point that can release you from your fears. In order to teach our children that we have a God worth worshipping, we need to reflect His attitudes. What we do and what we say need to show them what God is like. Sure, we'll miss the mark at times and we'll be very unlike God in the midst of many situations. But, start expressing these simple phrases and you will begin to build an open channel of communication within your family and to usher in an atmosphere in your home that points to our Father.

"I love you." You can't express love too much. These three words bring assurance and confidence to the spirit of any child. Use this sentence liberally. No matter if it's one of those sweet moments when it seems natural or if it's in the midst of one of those infamous power struggles, express your love. *Especially* when they aren't all that lovable, kids need to hear that they are loved. Remember the wonder of discovering that while we were still sinners, Christ died for us? As we demonstrate grace, we build something positive into the spirits of our children.

How Does God Feel About Questions?

Lead a family discussion on the topic, "How does God feel about questions?" Direct the conversation toward the fact that God isn't mad at us or scared, because we have questions. He wants to demonstrate His love and His power in the midst of them. This discussion can reveal those areas in which family members themselves are questioning God. Like God, we need not be alarmed, but, instead, we have an opportunity to know how we can pray for them and gently guide them. End your time together in prayer.

"I'm proud of you." Nothing affirms someone's abilities and sense of purpose and belonging more than these simple words. The phrase is readily accessible to us when our kids accomplish something big, and rightfully so. But the expression's fullest effect is wielded when we acknowledge things that might not be as obvious. Good decisions that are made under pressure or wholehearted efforts that fail to produce a glowing success require a worthy response along these lines, "Though the rest of the world might not know it at the moment, you deserve to know that I'm proud of you." And, with the simplest reason of all, "I'm proud of you because you're my kid," our children learn our love and acceptance of them has nothing to do with what they do, but who they are. And isn't that a beautiful picture of God's love for us!

"I'm sorry" and "I forgive you." Apologies and forgiveness are contagious. That's why, in His Word, God speaks to us time and time again about giving and receiving forgiveness. The heartfelt expressions of "I'm sorry" and "I forgive you" are foundational to maintaining relationships. When a parent takes the lead, it creates not only a peaceful atmosphere in the home, but it models a relationship with God that encourages unhindered worship.

"Pray for me." It is scriptural to agree in prayer with your family about things each of you are facing. And, it teaches a valuable lesson about where to turn in the midst of challenges and difficulties. God is faithful. As He meets our families' needs and answers our prayers, a lesson is learned, and worship is the natural response.

Relax! You don't need all the answers! In the midst of honest communication, you'll begin to build trust within the walls of your home. Trust creates connections, and connections create confidence. That's exactly the atmosphere we want to be evident in our home. And, those are exactly the qualities we want to develop in our worship.

When we come into a personal relationship with Jesus, His complete forgiveness of our sins and total acceptance of us as His children bring a sense of freedom and release that are the source of a lifetime of abiding peace and abundant joy. Being truly *"accepted in the Beloved"* (Ephesians 1:6 NKJV) is the most basic joy of our salvation. We no longer need to play games with God or games with ourselves regarding God.

This is the very heart of what we want our family members to understand about their own relationships with Him. For them to come to such an understanding, they must be able to see that we are not perfect, but we are allowing ourselves to be redeemed in an ongoing process of becoming like Jesus.

If we make it seem that the process is complete, that every answer is in place, and that we never have to overcome obstacles or grapple with answers to honest questions, then we actually place a heavy burden on our children's lives. It will appear to them that they must have it all together and have every question answered before they can come to God. How tragic! God, and His work in people, is not a simple fairy tale, told to make children believe in antiseptic happy endings. Walking with God, knowing and loving and serving Him, is a process, one that is exciting and fulfilling and messy and challenging. If we honestly allow our children to observe us as we participate, we will allow them to see the reality of the God we love and serve, and they will be drawn to Him.

On My Heart, On His Heart

Prepare discussion prompts that can be presented during meals, while traveling, or at other occasions when you find the family gathered together. Present a topic and have each person finish the sentence. The topics should reveal personal thoughts, feelings, struggles, and victories, as each family member is encouraged to share from their hearts. Here are some suggestions for prompts:

- "I need God to..."
- "If I could change one thing in my life right now, it would be..."
- "I'm feeling really good about..."
- "I thank God for [Mom, Dad, Brother, or Sister] because..."

End your discussion time in prayer.

Stone upon Stone

In the home where you grew up, was the prevailing atmosphere one of transparency or one of privacy about spiritual matters? How is that affecting your openness with your own family?

Do your actions and attitudes at home reveal that your faith in God is practical and observable?

How could family members benefit from observing your struggles as well as your triumphs as a follower of Christ?

What is healthy about allowing your family to see that Christians have doubts, questions, and obstacles to overcome? How is it healthy for the rest of the world to see that Christians wrestle with difficult issues?

"This is how much God loved the world: He gave his Son, his one and only Son. And this is why: so that no one need be destroyed; by believing in him, anyone can have a whole and lasting life. God didn't go to all the trouble of sending his Son merely to point an accusing finger, telling the world how bad it was. He came to help, to put the world right again."
—John 3:16–17 (*The Message*)

5

Navigating Cultural Currents

Martha offers fresh ideas that can help us focus on God in the midst of today's culture, but first, Greg takes us back to the 1970s and admits he still has a fog machine ready to dust off for just the right occasion. Thankfully, he has lost his big Afro hairdo, long sideburns, and that lime-green polyester leisure suit.

Churches of all denominations are facing a dilemma today. Young adults have been abandoning the church at an alarming rate. According to LifeWay Research, 70 percent of young adults stopped attending church for at least a year at some point following their graduation from high school. Young adults offered plenty of excuses as to why they made this decision. But, like the student whose dog ate his homework, those excuses seemed somewhat flimsy. Scott McConnell, associate director of LifeWay Research, says, "To remain in church, a person must have experienced the value of the teaching and relationships at church and see the relevance for the next phase of life."

The very same thing could be said about how that spiritual connection happens in our home. Some parents might recoil at the suggestion that we change the way we teach our children to be worshippers. But, these same folks might see the priority of missionaries to a foreign land learning the native language and immersing themselves in that new culture. The fact is, today's homes are as foreign to the parents' upbringing as a developing country may be to an American missionary. Though God never changes, our culture changes so dramatically that we need to revise our ways of teaching our children the truth about God and who He is.

This isn't a new challenge.

I was just out of college back in 1976. The excitement of the Jesus Movement, an amazing move of God that swept across the country, was beginning to settle somewhat. And, I was anticipating how I might move on to inspire young lives to even bigger and better things in their walks with God.

I sat across the desk from a prominent youth pastor—my personal youth ministry guru—as he assessed for me the current youth culture. All youth pastors, at that time, were basking in the glory of one of the most significant revivals among youth in history. And the good ones were looking ahead as to how the church would grab the attention of the next wave of seekers.

"These teens are different than we've ever seen before," he said. "When you stand up before them and try to talk to them, they seem to look right through you."

He called them the non-responsive generation. He said that it was the first wave of teens whose lives had been totally immersed in television. Television was not just a pastime for them. It was their amusement, their educator, their babysitter, and their best friend. They didn't need to interact with anyone, because their television was there to entertain them.

Unfortunately, when a live person stood before them in a youth meeting or a classroom, they were conditioned to look right through them. "When you ask them a question," my youth pastor friend said, "they just stare at you blankly and never offer an answer."

A roomful of fresh faces simply staring back at you is a youth pastor's nightmare. Having now worked with teens most of my adult life, I can tell you assuredly, we youth ministers can be a somewhat insecure lot. If we don't hear the laughter, if there are no tears, or if, God forbid, one of those kids falls asleep, we can instantly be reduced to a quivering mass of frail fallibility.

"What do we need to do to reach these kids?" He asked me a question that I knew he had already thought through, so I, just like the teens in his youth group, sat back and waited for him to dispense the answer. "We have to shock their senses." His solution, along with most other youth pastors of the day, was to go toe-to-toe with the pop culture, offering louder music, more lights, and anything bigger, better, and more outrageous to motivate these kids to worship.

Youth meetings were transformed into rock concert-like celebrations. Lights, noise, and, yes, even pyrotechnics, were employed. And, hallelujah! Kids responded! It is at this point that I must reluctantly admit that I bought a fog machine to enhance my communication with the kids. I envisioned the eerie smoke pouring over the stage, illuminated by brilliant lighting, as the band led the teens in the latest Scripture choruses set to a rock beat. For a while, my vision worked beautifully. The kids actually began to participate, and they gave our youth meetings the official "cool" stamp of approval.

The war had begun, and we were determined to fight this battle with the world and win!

The rude awakening came when we youth workers realized that church youth budgets weren't nearly as deep as the entertainment industry's. Try as we might, we just couldn't go toe-to-toe with their high-tech toys. The bigger and louder we got, they still out-flashed us. They were always a step ahead, more outrageous and more extrasensory. Then MTV came along, and the world would never be the same again. Finally, with the influx of this round-the-clock dazzle, we had to surrender. It was time to regroup. No match for the flashy culture of the early 1980s, I packed up the fog machine (which now gathers dust in an isolated corner of my shed, waiting for a comeback), unplugged the technology, and whimpered in the corner, wondering if the old, old story would ever be relevant to youthful ears again.

Culture Shift

But, time passed by, and, alas, the popular culture soon began changing too. We should have seen it coming, because style moves in cycles. I never throw away a wild, wide tie or a leisure suit, because I just know someday I'll see it again in *GQ*.

MTV's loud and brash video playlist became boring and repetitive in the eyes of young viewers. Programming executives were desperate not only to read the culture, but to drive it. They observed a building immunity to all the flash and noise. They anticipated a surge of interest in more interactive, less brash pursuits—the coming Internet—and they began to sense a new trend. They gathered their marketing geniuses, who began to analyze and strategize. At first, their efforts to engage the new youth were subtle. A series of name-your-favorite-artist "unplugged" concerts were new and interesting—and quieter. Amazingly, the kids gravitated to the more personal, less in-your-face approach. The concept made the audience members feel more a part of what was going on. They weren't just being entertained; they were involved.

Finally, the television gurus turned a corner as MTV began to hype *The Real World*, a show that focuses on the interpersonal relationships of seven strangers living in one house. Thus, reality television—a voyeuristic peek into the lives of other people—was born!

The amazing success of *The Real World* spawned other programs of the same genre, and today, the top-rated shows on television fall into the reality category. Networks are scrambling to be even more "real" and pushing the envelope to become even more raw. "So you want real life?" they seem to be saying. "Get a load of this!" Television offers shows about real people meeting and marrying, finding a job, aspiring to be superstars, swapping lives and wives, putting up with rowdy kids, and simply just interacting. What began as a cultural current has become a tidal wave.

Cultural change is inevitable. Its ebb and flow makes for some interesting cycles in our world's history. And, though we may often resist it, these changes are, more often than not, actually a blessing. It keeps life exciting! Every generation has battled cultural trends.

Engaging the Culture

Perhaps the most crucial aspect of guiding our children to real, personal, lifelong relationships with God is helping them to make connections between what they read in the Bible and hear at church and what they see and experience in the culture in which we live.

If we can create opportunities to talk about issues before a moment of personal crisis arises in our one of our children's lives, our guidance will be much more effective. Those preemptive conversations are more reason-driven than emotion-driven.

So it is a good idea, beginning in earliest childhood and continuing right on through the teens and early twenties, to use the media, the arts, and current events to discuss cultural ideas and situations in light of applicable biblical principles.

Read books, watch movies, go to museums, listen to the news, attend concerts and plays, and then talk about them. Ask your children open-ended questions about the characters, the conflicts, and the themes, and really listen to what they say. Share your ideas, as well, being careful to express them as ideas, rather than edicts.

Not only does such dialogue teach your children to think and to apply a Christ-like worldview for themselves, but such discussions also create an open door for trusting communication when the children's conflicts with the culture take on a personal nature.

Here's a very brief list of ideas on how to engage the culture as a family "when you sit in your house," and when you "walk by the way." (See Deuteronomy 6:7 NKJV.)

 Read all seven of *The Chronicles of Narnia* by C. S. Lewis. Find and talk about biblical themes. This is great for all ages, even adults!

 Watch the 2002 version of *The Count of Monte Cristo* (PG-13) with your teens. Discuss the situations in the movie in light of sound, godly principles and symbols.

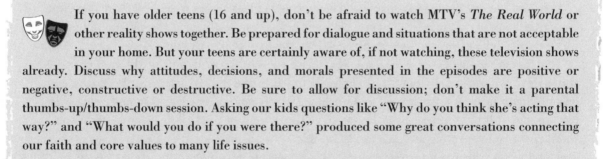 If you have older teens (16 and up), don't be afraid to watch MTV's *The Real World* or other reality shows together. Be prepared for dialogue and situations that are not acceptable in your home. But your teens are certainly aware of, if not watching, these television shows already. Discuss why attitudes, decisions, and morals presented in the episodes are positive or negative, constructive or destructive. Be sure to allow for discussion; don't make it a parental thumbs-up/thumbs-down session. Asking our kids questions like "Why do you think she's acting that way?" and "What would you do if you were there?" produced some great conversations connecting our faith and core values to many life issues.

 National news networks provide an excellent forum for talking about world events with your family. Knowing the day's news also offers opportunities to pray together for world leaders and people in crisis.

Had the shock trends of the 1980s continued, today we would be attempting the impossible task of grabbing the attention of nonresponsive teenage zombies. Thankfully, there still seems to be a limit to the physical and emotional sensitivities of human beings. Nevertheless, kids today react and learn differently than their parents did and differently than those kids in my early youth groups as well.

Marc Prensky is an acclaimed writer and speaker with a visionary insight into education and the way children learn. In his article "Digital Natives, Digital Immigrants," which appeared in the journal *On the Horizon* (October 2001), Prensky identifies this generation as "digital natives." They are the first to be, from the womb, totally immersed in computers, video games, cell phones, digital cameras, and all the peripheral technology that goes along with it. The kids of today spend less than half as much time reading as they spend watching television, playing video games, and surfing the Internet. Prensky believes the digital environment has radically altered the way today's children learn. He postulates that the actual structure of their brains has been changed to the point that there is no getting back to learning the way it used to be.

In the past, learning took place by reading, absorbing, and reciting. Though that method should never be completely abandoned, today's learners are not accustomed to such a one-dimensional introduction of information. They respond more to breadth than depth. Our challenge is to disseminate the truth to our children in as many ways as we possibly can. Kids today love variety. A mixed bag of methods will always grab their attention. Then, when they find the one formula that appeals to them, they are motivated to stop there and dig a little deeper. Consider the way people surf the Internet. We move from site to site, accumulating information, then, one place in particular draws us in further. That's the way digital natives make connections.

In order to effectively reach our kids, we may need to rethink some old ideas. Our typical "Christian viewpoint" may have evolved into some things that we, and, more importantly, God, never intended it to become.

We don't need to fear integrating today's technology or styles of learning into our teaching . Fear was never what God intended for us in our relationship with the changing world. We're a part of this planet, and God created us and placed us right here, right now for a distinct purpose – to bring glory to Him. We have a responsibility to magnify God so that He fills the emptiness in people and their hopeless situations, which we see all around us. Technology can, and should be, redeemed for His purposes.

A Mission in the World

John 17 is one of the most intimate accounts of Jesus's life on earth. It is His prayer to His Father. His heart is exposed, and He discloses His desires and hopes for His ministry and His followers. Jesus's plan and His purpose for His people are revealed.

Wired!

Long before computers were as common as cook stoves in American homes, Marshall McLuhan said "the medium is the message." While our message surely transcends that discussion, making use of the digital age is a good way to make our family worship more relevant to our children's lives.

 Draw names among family members, secret-pal style, and then text message a Bible verse or a prayer to one another at some time during the week.

 Each day let every person in the family email all the others one reason why God is worthy of praise. At the end of the week, copy and paste all of it into one document, print it, and hang it on the fridge. You can even get creative by adding photos and clip art.

 Create a family blog and post stories about God's interaction with you as individuals or as a family. This will not only be an altar in your home, but it could become a place of worship for others across the world!

 Let the kids write and produce a family worship podcast.

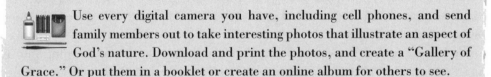 Use every digital camera you have, including cell phones, and send family members out to take interesting photos that illustrate an aspect of God's nature. Download and print the photos, and create a "Gallery of Grace." Or put them in a booklet or create an online album for others to see.

Latecomers to the digital scene may need to ask for help with this one. Parents can surprise their kids by downloading some current Christian music (the kids' style, not the parents') onto the kids' MP3 players, to encourage them toward personal worship in those moments when kids are "alone" with their music.

(continued)

"Now I'm returning to you. I'm saying these things in the world's hearing so my people can experience my joy completed in them. I gave them your word; the godless world hated them because of it, because they didn't join the world's ways, just as I didn't join the world's ways. I'm not asking that you take them out of the world but that you guard them from the Evil One. They are no more defined by the world than I am defined by the world. Make them holy—consecrated—with the truth; your word is consecrating truth. In the same way that you gave me a mission in the world, I give them a mission in the world. I'm consecrating myself for their sakes, so they'll be truth-consecrated in their mission."
—John 17:13–19 (*The Message*)

Within the context of this prayer, Jesus revealed some timeless principles concerning a believer's connection with the culture.

Our perspective may seldom be in harmony with our culture. The world doesn't comprehend a Christian worldview. They couldn't even if they wanted to, because their frame of reference is completely opposed to that of a Christian. They do not have the Spirit within them.

"The world cannot accept him, because it neither sees him nor knows him. But you know him, for he lives with you and will be in you."
—John 14:17 (NIV)

Jesus said in John 17 that the world actually has a hatred for the things of God. We see that demonstrated in various degrees and tracks. It can be subtle or venomous. It's not confined to a particular ideology or political persuasion. It is simply that unregenerate minds cannot mesh with the indwelling Spirit of God in believers.

We made sure that our kids, from a young age, knew that they were different from others in the world. We never wanted them to see themselves as superior,

Wired!

If you have a digital video camera, shoot a music video to illustrate a favorite praise song or a Bible verse. This can be an ongoing project, as you talk through concepts for the lyrics, plan the shots, set up, and shoot the scenes (on location, perhaps). Then, download the video, edit it, add the sound, and so forth. You could even post your finished product on www.youtube.com or www.Godtube.com an alternative for Christians.

As part of your Bible study time, use the computer to check out www.biblegateway.com, which shows numerous English translations, along with other languages, side by side for comparison. Also, http://net.bible.org/home.php is another great online tool, with commentaries and Bible dictionaries.

Come visit us! We're online at www.settingupstones.com. You can get ideas and be inspired, or you can share your ideas and be an inspiration.

Back to the Bible: Paul Goes Greek

As Paul walked the streets of Athens, he must have been troubled by the rampant idolatry he observed. The Greeks had gods for every occasion; their culture had produced a theological nightmare. Whenever they felt a need to bring some order and meaning to a particular part of their lives, they would invent a new god, attribute power and wisdom to it, and build a place where they could worship it. The result was that the territories of individual Greek gods began to overlap, provoking continual debate about which deity controlled what. Even the most brilliant philosophers of the day threw up their hands as they attempted to untangle this religious mess. So, just to be safe, they invented "an unknown god" and reasoned that would take care of everything.

Paul's first instinct may have been to blast them for the unholy circus they had created, or maybe he was tempted to write them off as unredeemable. But he knew that, because of their pride and self-righteousness, the Greeks wouldn't respond well to a frontal assault. And Paul also knew that God loved these people too much to release him from revealing His truth to them. So, as he stood before the Athenians to speak, Paul used something from their very own culture, idolatrous as it was, to introduce them to Almighty God.

(continued)

but, instead, we wanted them to know they are in the midst of being changed into Christ's likeness. We wanted them to expect that they would have different ideas about things. We cautioned them that they shouldn't be shocked when someone disagreed with them or tried to convince them that their viewpoint was wrong.

We aren't defined by our culture. Our culture will attempt to compartmentalize believers. They will stereotype us and label us. We are all too often characterized by our imperfections, as if failures automatically prove hypocrisy. Unfortunately, we may have brought some of this on ourselves through self-righteousness and judgmental attitudes. But, in fact, Jesus is clear that the perceived enlightenment of the culture in no way proves or disproves our status in God's eyes. So, measuring ourselves against the standards set by the world is futile.

Isolation is not the answer, however. I have sensed a trend in the church in recent years that disturbs me. An attitude of fear has brought about isolationism. We have a generation of children that has never been challenged or jostled, so they are distressed when the inevitable cultural confrontations occur. Jesus spoke clearly to His Father, "My prayer is not that you take them out of the world" (John 17:15). He never intended that we hide out or hunker down. We are supposed to rub shoulders with the world, mix with them and talk to them. In His world, Jesus wasn't known as a "holy man," but as "the carpenter." He interacted with His culture and was involved in His community.

We don't need to fear our culture. We sometimes find ourselves fearful of being overwhelmed by negative influences. We flee. We take cover. We tremble. "Greater is He that is in you than he that is in the world" (1 John 4:4 KJV). Those are powerful words. But, for their truth to be realized in our daily lives, we must allow God to provide the protection. I don't know about you, but even at my strongest, my strength can't rival the protection of Almighty God!

Setting Up Stones

We have a mission to influence our culture. We have a divine purpose to be salt and light here. I'm thankful for the promise for eternal life in Heaven, but if that were the only reason we were saved, then there would be no reason to continue life here on earth. We aren't all called to proclaim the gospel from pulpits or from street corners. But we are all called to be witnesses, to reflect Jesus through our lives, which have been bought by His blood. In love, in actions and in words our story of redemption has the power to bring glory to God and life to our world.

God's perspective here is really not difficult. As baffling as the culture can be, His viewpoint, as always, is constant. In the midst of the things of this world that might hurt us, confuse us, or make us angry, God seeks simply to restore what is His. His creation— the beauty of vast expanses of nature, the majesty of the seas and the skies, the diverse varieties of people—belongs to Him. The enemy has sought to steal it, kill it and destroy it, but God simply desires to win it back, purify it, and put it in order. Redemption is what God is all about.

So just how does all this affect how we worship in our home? First it serves as a reminder that a life of worship isn't confined within our walls. Worship is vital. It is neither sterile nor stagnant. What we practice at home should saturate our lives and permeate our culture. That's what makes our relationship with God alive. We need not expect that the worship lifestyle we bring into the world will be fully accepted. Even when we see trends that might indicate more receptivity, there will always be spiritual barriers.

Back to the Bible: Paul Goes Greek

"Men of Athens! I see that in every way you are very religious. For as I walked around and looked carefully at your objects of worship, I even found an altar with this inscription: TO AN UNKNOWN GOD. *Now what you worship as something unknown I am going to proclaim to you.*

The God who made the world and everything in it is the Lord of heaven and earth and does not live in temples built by hands."
—Acts 17:22–24

These are the realities about our world that we teach our families. Though we should never place our children in harm's way, we must not isolate them so that they become fearful. Even more important, we must allow them freedom so that they can become effective in their own calling. God modeled the attitude that we are to have toward the world. He loved the world. He wasn't enamored by its philosophies and points of view. But He loved the people. He longed for their redemption and fellowship.

We can't escape our culture, because we're a part of it. And, we can learn to use the good, the bad, and the ugly of the world as tools to teach our families about God, because He's active in the world too. We discovered that asking our kids questions about their world gave us unlimited opportunities to point to God's activity all around them. *What*

Thinking It Through

The idea of "being in the world but not of the world" is sometimes controversial and certainly not an easy topic to define and apply to everyday living. It's important for us to understand what the prevailing ideas of our culture are and what motivates people to do what they do or say what they say. Several excellent books have been written on the subject and can provide valuable insights for Christians. These books aren't for family discussion but are worthwhile for your personal spiritual growth and understanding.

Some we'd recommend:

Breaking the Missional Code, Ed Stetzer and David Putman

Velvet Elvis: Repainting the Christian Faith, Rob Bell

The Three Hardest Words in the World to Get Right, Leonard Sweet

Go Fish, Andy Stanley

Intentional Living, Andrea Jones Mullins

does God think of this? Why? What should our attitude be? These questions have evolved into a strategy of cultural engagement for our family. The foundation is two-fold: we want to love the people around us, and we want to be confident in what we believe. The strategy requires constant communication and consistent acknowledgement of God's power and love. But our entire family can now see God at work in even the most difficult situations.

This culture is not our enemy. Satan is. He uses weak and willing people to accomplish his mission of stealing, killing and destroying. But, Jesus hasn't given up on this culture. He desires to bring redemption here and now. He longs to use our families and us as the channels through which the world can know Him and the peace, joy, love, and power He offers to all.

Stone upon Stone

Are your thoughts and actions as a family being driven by fear or by faith?

What is God's perspective concerning your world? How might your viewpoint be different from His?

How can you determine what aspects of today's culture are not healthy? How can you protect your family from those things? (Ephesians 6:10–18; Psalm 91)

How can you know what aspects of the culture are redeemable? How can you use them in setting up stones in our home? (John 17)

What can you learn from the way Jesus related to His culture and how can you apply it to the way you should relate to yours today? (Matthew 14:14)

A father to the fatherless, a defender of widows, is God in his holy dwelling. God sets the lonely in families, he leads forth the prisoners with singing.
—Psalm 68:5–6

6

Dealing with Different

Before moving on to some specific aspects of worship in section two, Martha and Greg address nontraditional families. Martha first acknowledges the variety of family situations in today's culture and investigates how God worked in "different" families in the Bible. Greg then relates the story of a blended family that made worship work in their home. While some of the content relates specifically to nontraditional settings, they also include principles that apply to all families.

In our world today, there are endless combinations of people living under one roof. In your house, there might be mom and two kids, or dad, grandma and four kids, or three single roommates, or mom, auntie and three cousins, or a blended family of yours, mine and ours, or a couple who have no children, or a couple whose children are out on their own. Or, the list may even change from week to week, as children and stepchildren move in and out according to a judge's orders. In fact, a survey done by the National Opinion Research Center concluded that the traditional family-structure model of a stay-at-home mother, working father, and children will become the minority this century.

It is interesting to note that God's words to Joshua and His people don't refer specifically to "family," as in people related by blood or marriage. He tells them to take the stones and set them up, literally, in "the place where you stay tonight" (Joshua 4:3).

No matter who lives under your roof, the goal is the same: to draw each separately and all together to worship God. With that said, however, there is an extra challenge for those

Creative Connections

While today's lifestyles make finding time for the whole family to meet together to worship a challenge for all families, it's even more difficult where only one adult is responsible for everything. But a little thought and creativity can help even the busiest, most scattered of families draw together to draw near to God. Sometimes, it's almost impossible to get everyone in the same place, at the same time to focus on God. The concept here, though, is to find ways to share a moment with God and each other, even when you're not together. Every parent treasures a card or note with "I love you" scribbled on it. It makes a connection even without face-to-face time. We're all wired that way, even your kids. Words, however communicated, mean something. Don't forget that whatever your family circumstances, your home was custom-made to give God glory!

You've Got Mail

Everyone loves mail, whether it's old-school postal mail or something personal in the email inbox. Each family member can write notes to the others, describing how they see God's handiwork in the others' lives and how God blesses them through the others. In just the few seconds it takes to pass out the letters and rip open the envelopes, or open the online mailbox, these notes can create a moment when, even if you're not side-by-side, together you lift your hearts toward Him.

(continued)

who find themselves solely responsible for a household. Having to earn a living, prepare the meals, keep the house, oversee the homework, and taxi kids as a one-person operation means that perhaps the biggest hurdle to family worship is finding time to gather everyone together. While the chapters that follow offer tips and ideas and practical guidelines, it is good to remember that this is not about adding tasks to the day. Rather, it is about creating an atmosphere in the place where you live that points people toward God.

God has worked in nontraditional homes before. He never changes, even when living situations do. The poignant story of Ruth and Naomi reveals how God isn't baffled by circumstances. Naomi's daughters-in-law were from another culture and another faith. That, alone, presented this family with some unusual challenges.

Naomi and her husband and sons had settled in Moab to escape the famine in their homeland. There, the sons married Moabite women, Ruth and Orpah. The household was already beginning to take on a different look for everyone. Then Naomi's husband died, followed by both of her sons. She was left in this foreign country with her daughters-in-law.

Something in Naomi's home had made an impact on Ruth and Orpah. When Naomi decided to move back to Judah, she released her daughters-in-law to return to their people, but both of them wanted to stay. And, while Orpah finally returned, Ruth made an impassioned commitment to her mother-in-law.

"Don't ask me to leave you and turn back. Wherever you go, I will go; wherever you live, I will live. Your people will be my people, and your God will be my God."
—Ruth 1:16 (NLT)

Despite her great grief, Naomi created a place where Ruth could know God and dwell in His presence. Naomi didn't abandon her faith in the middle of trials. She continued in her dedication to God and to making Him known in her home. She taught Ruth of His ways, counseling and encouraging her in her growing relationship with Him.

And God came through. He honored Naomi's faithfulness by restoring her joy and providing a redeemer for their family, Boaz, who married Ruth. Boaz and Ruth's son, Obed, was a forefather of David, and the Redeemer of the whole world, Jesus.

Though Naomi's circumstances made her home different, she purposed in her heart to make it a place of worship. It wasn't easy for Naomi, but the result made her diligence worthwhile.

> ## Creative Connections
> *Sticky-note Praise*
> Give everyone in the family a different colored pad of sticky notes. Instruct them to make note of things that they are thankful for, reasons to praise God, or a Bible verse, and stick the thought on headboards, mirrors, the TV, the fridge, or another appropriate place. Then, the next one to come along and find it will join in the thought. Though the time and place are not the same, the sentiment and prayer will link them together.

Sometimes the family structure in the home may be traditional, but the spiritual unity is missing. That can create situations that make building a worshipful home a difficult task.

We are introduced to Timothy in the sixteenth chapter of Acts. There, we read that Timothy's mother, Eunice, was a Jewish believer, and his father was Greek and didn't share her faith. Paul observed the promise within the young man's life and the maturity of his faith, which was well known in the community, and took him under his wing. Later, in a letter written to Timothy, Paul recognizes the spiritual foundation that was laid in Timothy's life by his mother Eunice and his grandmother Lois.

Eunice may have been badgered by her husband at every attempt to raise their son as a man of faith. Or, Timothy's father may have just completely withdrawn himself from that part of his life, choosing to throw up his hands and declare that he didn't want any part of that. Whatever the atmosphere, Eunice and her mother made a decision that their home would welcome the presence of God and that Timothy would know Him and see Him at work.

The process and principles we discuss in the following chapters do not change with your living arrangements. This book is not about a formula. It's about a daily dialogue, a redeeming of the ordinary for the extraordinary experience of making true worship the hallmark of our lives and the lives of those around us.

Focus on the Possible!

Instead of focusing on what isn't possible for our families at holidays and other traditional times, let's place our emphasis on what *is* possible!

On the first Christmas after Greg's dad died, a variety of circumstances combined to leave just our son, Greg's mom, and the two of us to celebrate Christmas Eve and Christmas Day. In prior years our house had been full of family.

Rather than sit and be sad about how things had changed, we decided to visit a candlelight carol service in a lovely old church in downtown San Antonio. The novelty of that service and the fact that the worship style was somewhat unfamiliar to us, somehow heightened the meaning of every carol and Bible verse. Right there, where others had worshipped beginning almost two centuries before, we shared one of the most meaningful Christmases we had ever had. Then, the four of us enjoyed the Christmas lights on the Riverwalk and dined on enchiladas at one of San Antonio's landmark restaurants.

The next day, we invited almost everyone we knew, and particularly people who were likely to be alone, to an open house. We had wall-to-wall people in every room, watching football, playing board games, singing karaoke, eating, talking, and laughing. We had to agree that it had ended up being one of the sweetest holiday times ever.

Instead of focusing on what we can't do, or what we don't have, and feeling somehow excluded from various traditional family celebrations, we can minister to both ourselves and others by reaching out and inviting others to join us.

New Family, New Opportunities

After a difficult divorce, Christine found herself as the single parent of three children, one in high school, one in middle school, and one early in elementary school. There were other circumstances, too, that made the situation even more challenging. Christine's ex-husband had been in the ministry, and in that position, her divorce had been very visible, and as a result, even more uncomfortable. The three beautiful children had been adopted, each brought into Christine's and her former husband's care from previous living situations that were abhorrent. She had loved them and nurtured them through many complicated adjustments. But now, she was concerned that the turmoil in her own home might shatter the children's naturally fragile hearts.

She turned to the only place she knew to find real strength and courage. Rather than isolating herself from the church, she wholeheartedly involved her family in fellowship with

Setting Up Stones

other believers where they received love and support. And, she purposefully made her home a place where the presence of God was welcome and could minister peace. She modeled God's nature through her consistency, and her determination to draw close to God witnessed to her children of His faithfulness. Her perseverance was rewarded as her family's commitment to their faith and their love for each other and for God grew.

A few years later, Christine renewed a friendship with Clayton, who she had known from her college days. As they spent time getting to know each other again, they began to share their hearts and their hopes, and they fell in love. In reaching a decision to be married, they considered all that Christine's children had been through in their brief lives.

As the time for their wedding drew closer, Clayton began to realize his responsibilities in this new family, and he purposed to do his part to continue the healing and growing process in the children's lives. He gathered the children to tell them of the plans that he and their mother had. Then, he set up stones in this new blended home. Clayton presented a ring to each child and told them that the ring symbolized not only the love that he had for their mom and his commitment to her, but, also, his obligation before God to them. He told them of his determination to provide love and support for them. And, he assured them that their home would be a safe place and sanctuary, where they could grow in their love and trust of God.

Establishing the kind of foundation that Christine and Clayton did generates an environment where worship can become an ongoing process. As worship is recognized as a way of life in your home, then everyone under your same roof will begin to catch that vision. They begin to share in the responsibility of finding ways and opportunities to worship God. When you choose to set the tone, worship will become a way of life for the whole family.

First Steps to Worship

Here are three steps that may help you establish a habit of worship for your home, no matter what your situation.

Be prepared. The first is to prepare yourself to be a worshipper. Search your heart for any fragment of bitterness, hurt, resentment, anger, disappointment, or frustration . . . toward another person, toward yourself, or toward God. Allow your heavenly Father to bring healing to your heart, soul, thoughts and emotions. We all must humble ourselves before the One who knows us best and loves us most. And we need to train our hearts to thank Him for who He is and what He has done for us, in order to have hearts that want to worship Him.

Be purposeful. Dragging those boulders from the riverbed to their tents took strong determination and stamina by the Hebrew fathers, as they strained their muscles, skinned hands and knuckles, and poured sweat into the ground. We must determine that we will "set up stones" and invest the effort to plan significant, meaningful times of worship for our households. The time need not be long, but it must be effective and engaging. The biggest part of the battle is resolving that your home will be a place of worship and continually partnering with God to make that happen. The purpose of the following chapters is to give you practical ideas on how to do just that.

Be perceptive. Finally, we must become constantly aware of those teachable moments that arise unexpectedly and grab any opportunity to direct our family's thoughts and hearts toward God. We must consistently bring attention to every occasion where He reveals His power and His love. We are determining to take a fresh look at what we call worship. It's usually rather easy to take notice of the big things God does for us. But finding Him in the simple things, the everyday events, is the way to make worship a natural occurrence.

Certainly, different often does mean difficult. Your situation at home may be extreme, and people and responsibilities are constantly demanding your time and attention. But, this is where you are, and it's vitally important to live in the present and make every moment count. As you determine to create an atmosphere of worship right now, opportunities will arise naturally because you are utilizing every day's experiences to offer worship to God. Once you purpose in your heart to do so, it won't be long before those unexpected moments begin to flow into a ceaseless, refreshing, renewing fountain of worship from your home to the very heart of God.

Stone upon Stone

Have you allowed any anger, bitterness, or resentment to take root in your life? How could that affect your spiritual health and your ability to set a tone of worship in your home? (Hebrews 12:14–15)

Even though you're busy, what are some ways you can rearrange things so that setting up stones can be a priority in your home?

What times of the day or week is everyone in your household available? How can you use those times to make your home a place of worship?

Building the
Altar of Worship

"As for me and my family, we'll worship God."
—Joshua 24:15 (*The Message*)

Let the Word of Christ—the Message—have the run of the house. Give it plenty of room in your lives. Instruct and direct one another using good common sense. And sing, sing your hearts out to God!
—Colossians 3:16 (*The Message*)

7

I've Got the Music in Me

Greg examines why music is such an important part of most people's worship experiences. But if it's such a good thing, why do so many people argue about it? Check out the sidebars where Martha has uncovered some resources that will help you find music that will draw the whole family into worship.

Remember a few chapters back, when we established the fact that worship is much more than the musical offerings that happen at church? OK, good. But let's not ignore the importance of music. While it is certainly true that worship is more than music, the significance of corporate worship in song should not be minimized. I would say some of my most memorable and moving worship experiences have occurred in exactly that setting. For my entire life, music has been the centerpiece of my expressions to God. My earliest memories are of singing in church—the sounds, the fervor, and the feeling.

Music is an expression of the soul. We could probably engage in a debate of the precise theological underpinnings of that statement. But, it should be noted that both the Old and New Testaments are filled with references to musical worship. From deep within, generation after generation has poured out praises to God in song. Music moves us, and music moves God.

Martin Luther was not only a theologian who changed the course of the history of religion. He was a prolific hymn writer, and some church historians claim that his music inspired the birth of congregational singing. He was passionate about music as an expression of worship and the power it held.

Music is one of the greatest gifts that God has given us: It is divine and therefore Satan is its enemy. For with its aid many dire temptations are overcome; the devil does not stay where music is.
—Martin Luther, *In Praise of Music*

God invented music, and He loves it. He created a way that, when a string is plucked or wind passes across a reed, the air vibrates and causes music. The very breath He breathed into our lungs is expelled across two pieces of flesh, called vocal cords, and we're singing. Think about these passages for a moment:

Come, let us sing for joy to the LORD; let us shout aloud to the Rock of our salvation. Let us come before him with thanksgiving and extol him with music and song.
—Psalm 95:1–2

Thank God! Call out his Name! Tell the whole world who he is and what he's done! Sing to him! Play songs for him! Broadcast all his wonders!
—1 Chronicles 16:8–9 (*The Message*)

"The LORD your God is with you, he is mighty to save. He will take great delight in you, he will quiet you with his love, he will rejoice over you with singing."
—Zephaniah 3:17

So if music is important to God, it certainly should be important to us. He created it, and He made it a vital part of our lives and our worship of Him. Music enhances our worship. It gives worship another dimension, another expression.

What makes music worshipful, then? Is it the lyrics? Do tones, chords, and sounds determine what's worship? Is there a certain rhythm or tempo that's more conducive to our worship?

C. S. Lewis was not a musician, and by some indications, was not particularly fond of music. He did, though, have definite ideas about music and its connection to worship. I think his insights remain significant for us:

It seems to me that we must define rather carefully the way, or ways, in which music can glorify God.... An excellently performed piece of music, as natural operation which reveals in a very high degree the peculiar powers given to man, will thus always glorify God whatever the intention of the performers may be. But that is a kind of glorifying which we share with the "dragons and great deeps," with the "frost and snows." What is looked for in us, as men, is another kind of glorifying, which depends on intention. How easy or how hard it may be for a whole choir to preserve that intention through all the discussions and decisions, all the corrections and the disappointments, all the temptations to pride, rivalry and ambition, which precede the performance of a great work, I (naturally) do not know. But it is on the intention that all depends. When it succeeds, I think the performers are the most enviable of men; privileged while mortals to honor God like angels and, for a few golden moments, to see spirit and flesh, delight and labour, skill and worship, the natural and the supernatural, all fused into that unity they would have had before the Fall.

—C. S. Lewis, "On Church Music," *Christian Reflections*

Lewis's conclusions, then, are that all music brings glory to God, because He created the music and the musician. By the intentions of the heart, however, true worship is defined. In his opinion, good music, no matter the style, glorifies God. But, good music in which the musician purposes to glorify God is worship. If we embrace that philosophy about music, then we probably have to adjust our traditional perceptions just a bit—or maybe a whole lot. The beauty of good music brings glory to God, no matter if it's a Christian song or not. It might even encourage an atmosphere of worship. Worship really happens, though, through songs that are intentional about bringing glory to God.

With all these questions and opinions, we've unearthed one of the most consistently troubling controversies in the history of the church. With every generation and in every faction and denomination, church leaders have taken a stance. Godly men and women have disagreed, and a certain rumbling has almost always been just below the surface, at times erupting into full-scale divisiveness. How unfortunate that something so good has become so disruptive.

Within our families, though, we must determine that we will make use of the value that music brings to our worship. We cannot allow it to cause conflict like it has on a broader scale. In order to do that, we have to establish some general principles about music in our homes and reach some conclusions about music and worship where even church leaders have failed.

All Ears

 Give the whole family about a week for each member to find some worship music on CDs that they enjoy. Then, come together and let each person play their music (one or two selections) for everyone else. After that, they can tell what they like about the music, its style, and its meaning, and what particular significance it has for them. Most ages will have something to share. This is not a time for the family critics to offer reviews, but an opportunity for everyone to share what music is significant to them.

Develop some guidelines about music in general. Everybody has a different opinion about what constitutes good music, and there is often a generational divide regarding certain styles and their merits. As your family grows and your children approach the teen years, you can almost be certain that there will be a confrontation about their music choices. A reasonable, honest and thoughtful discussion, though, should help bridge that great divide.

Of course, there are some songs that should be completely off-limits. Lyrics that are obscene or that promote activity that flies in the face of your family's values are not acceptable. However, there are ways of reaching an agreement with your child about this type of music without the because-I-said-so reasoning. Young children can understand explanations like, "That song says things that make God sad." As your child moves on into the teen years, an open and specific discussion about the lyrics is a valid way to handle the situation. A frank discussion is not threatening, and if the teen is honest with you and him or herself and agrees that the music is not relating a message that he or she embraces, then he or she becomes the one who is actually making the call.

As hard as you might try to guide your child's opinion about music, there may be times when no just means no. When you reach an impasse, though, make sure your decision is based on more than the fact that it's not your taste in music.

Let music create an atmosphere of worship in your home. During a typical day when your family's at home, stop what you're doing for a moment and just listen. If your home is like most, it's usually a pretty noisy place. The TV is blaring, people are yelling from room to room, doors are slamming, alarms of some kind or another are buzzing, video games are blasting, and some noises are audible but completely indefinable.

The Noise Pollution Clearinghouse (NPC) is a for-real national nonprofit organization that seeks to reduce noise pollution in homes, neighborhoods, cities, and wherever else the menace might be found. Had we only known about this organization when our kids were at home! We had to do our civic duty without NPC's help.

But, if given a choice between raucous noise or complete silence around our house, I would have to opt for noise. However, at times, even good things can get out of control. We

Educate Yourself

You can find family-friendly reviews of music, as well as movies and other entertainment, online at these sites:

• www.pluggedinonline.com
This is the online version of a printed magazine from Focus on the Family. The format is attractive to teens, and the wide range of subject matter includes every facet of the cultural spectrum.

• www.christiananswers.net/spotlight
Produced by Eden Communications, this is another excellent site that majors on the visual media. And the cool part is, there's a link so you can listen to Christian music while you browse around. It's part of a broader site at christiananswers.net.

decided that there would be occasions when we would declare a moratorium on all noise except music. Do you remember the story of the first encounter between Saul and David? David's music soothed Saul's anger and torment. What we discovered was that the music always set a peaceful tone in our house too. There were never as many arguments, and we all had more positive attitudes. Sometimes, it even ushered the family into a time of worshipping together.

You don't need to invest in a high-end sound system to accomplish your goal. A boom box works just fine. Build a collection of worship music that everyone in the family finds palatable, and, when times are stressful or unbelievably fast-paced, play a selection and drink in life and peace. God will take it from there.

Compromise, in this case, is not a bad thing. Our son Matt had the wonderful opportunity of serving on the staff at University Baptist Church in Waco, Texas, while he was attending college. There he ministered alongside David Crowder. Dave was one of the cofounders of the church when he was a college student in 1996, and now he is one of Christian music's most outstanding talents. The first time I met him, I probably stared, and I should apologize to him for that. Dave is very tall and very thin. I think gangly might be a better description. Basically, he's all arms and legs—with a whole lot of hair. He has a shock of hair atop his head that stands straight up, black horn-rims à la Buddy Holly, and facial hair that he claims is not actually a goatee, but whatever it is, it's certainly prominent. David Crowder is a unique dude. And his music is at least as different as he is. Christianity Today International's ChristianMusicToday.com calls his music "wildly creative" and "rock, folk, worship, pop, electronica, bluegrass . . . just like it'll be in heaven someday."

Matt introduced us to Dave and his music, and since he was so excited about it, I felt that I should at least indulge him. It's not the usual style of music that I embrace, but I listened to it and I began to love it. Now, the David Crowder Band is always on my playlist. I can't believe that there was a moment when I first heard this music that I was tempted to just walk away. David Crowder is a man after God's heart and his music undeniably and unashamedly reflects his passion. He is a worshipper.

For Your Listening Pleasure

These Web sites have extensive offerings of music and information for worship. You're sure to find something that appeals to everybody's taste and interest level!

• www.worshipmusic.com

You'll find absolutely anything you want in the way of worship music here, whether you're just a casual listener or a music professional.

• www.christianmusic.com

Whatever style of music you enjoy, there's a Christian musician who's playing it and you're sure to find it here. Pages of reviews are an extra bonus.

• www.worshipleader.com

If you're involved in worship music beyond the walls of your home, *Worship Leader* magazine offers this Web site of music selections, reviews, discussions, and encouragement.

O Praise Him (All This For a King)

Turn your ear	Turn your gaze
To heaven and hear	To heaven and raise
The noise inside	A joyous noise
The sound of angels' awe	The sound of salvation come
The sound of angels' songs	The sound of rescued ones
And all this for a King	And all this for a King
We could join and sing	Angels join to sing
All to Christ the King	All for Christ our King
How constant, how divine	Oh la, la, la, la, la, la
This song of ours will rise	
O, how constant, how divine	How infinite and sweet
This love of ours will rise	This love so rescuing
	O, how infinitely sweet
O praise Him	This great love that has redeemed
O praise Him	As one we sing
He is Holy	
He is Holy (yeah)	Alleluia
	Alleluia
	He is Holy
	He is Holy (yeah)

It's so easy to prejudge, especially when it comes to music. We hear a style that stretches us beyond our comfort level and we want to turn it off. Remember when you proclaimed that you would *never* end up being *that* kind of parent? But, if it's our desire to see our whole family become worshippers, then we have to allow each person to discover the music that moves them. And, then, we have to squelch the urge to complain about the sound or turn our noses up at their move toward worship. Encouragement is essential here. That means when the new CD from their favorite Christian artist is released, we're eager to finance the purchase. We have to remember that our children are not our clones. Each of us is a unique creation of God, in the process of being conformed to His image.

Setting Up Stones

Set the tone with tolerance. Allow every family member to enjoy their own expressions of worship through their music of choice. Christian music is the most diverse of any musical genre. It's like a diamond with many facets. Whatever your taste is, God has raised up a voice who worships that way. Be the one in your family who appreciates everybody else's style. By doing so, you will confirm that your family's efforts toward worship are good, and that will give them confidence to reach out for more. You may be surprised at the results too. In your efforts to affirm others, you might discover that your own worship is enhanced and expanded.

Make music together. I know exactly what you're thinking: *I can't even carry a tune, so how can I make music?* Scripture has already debunked that unfounded excuse. Seven times in the Book of Psalms (KJV), we're implored to *"make a joyful noise"* to the Lord. That phrase, from the original Hebrew, is also defined as a shout, a sound, a cry, or a blast. Not once does it imply that it has to be of performance quality or even in tune, for that matter. The Bible does have something to say about *how* the noise is presented. Besides the "joyful" that we read in Psalms, the noise is also supposed to be loud and triumphant, and that's the kind of music that anyone can make!

As our kids were growing up, their absolute favorite music was a series of children's worship recordings called *Bullfrogs and Butterflies* and *Music Machine*. The kids played those old cassettes so much that even I can still sing every song and never miss a beat! The recordings were produced by Fletch Wiley, one of the most outstanding musicians and producers/arrangers in Christian music. He has been nominated for four Grammy Awards and has won in one category. His music has also received acclaim from the Gospel Music Association, *Billboard*, and *Campus Life* (now *Ignite Your Faith*). His perspective on worship music is insightful and professional.

Fletch says the hesitancy that we have to sing out and make a joyful noise is more a cultural phenomenon than just human nature. He related a story to us about one of his many concert tours around the world:

> "In other countries, people are not so shy about singing to each other. I have been to Turkey on several musical mission trips. Once, we were traveling across Istanbul in a van, and we came across a group of college students who had just finished their

Time-Out!
Occasionally, especially when things have been a bit hectic, just call time-out! Bring your whole group together and let them know that it's time for everyone to be refreshed. Limit extraneous noise and put on a CD of worship music. Don't use the same music style every time, but vary it instead. It might even be a good idea to put together your own mix CD, with selections included from everybody's playlist.

finals. They were outside one of the buildings there, just serenading each other with folk songs and love songs. It was very sweet and musically pleasing.

A girl in our van asked me to sing one of our worship songs to the group. I couldn't, or maybe wouldn't, do it. I wasn't a great singer,—I was a trumpet and flute player— and I was inhibited unless I could really "deliver" the song in a professional way. I feigned shyness, which, by the way, is something we all just need to get over. How sad. To them it was a sign of a deflated soul, and, really, I couldn't agree more. We need to worship openly, without regard to our reputations or vocal prowess."

There's something unifying that happens when you make music with other people. Singers and musicians will speak of a closeness that occurs, when, within the discipline of notes and lyrics, they create music together.

Fletch discussed with us about how important it was that his family took opportunities to sing together. "We sang all styles of music in our home, and I think it really had a wonderful effect on our children as they grew up and went out into the world. I think singing together as a family is a ritual, almost a habit, which should be cultivated, nurtured, and enjoyed," he said. "It is a powerful expression of our love to God. And, when our family hears the music and words coming out of our own mouths, it will change us."

Maybe it's simply that joining together in one spirit, one heart, and one mind to make music creates a oneness and draws people together. But, even more likely, voices and instruments raised together in worship move the heart of God and, as Psalm 22:3 (KJV) says, He inhabits the praises of His people. Whatever the reason that music changes us, when our families worship together in song we can be sure to experience a connection. It's not a new thing. Generation after generation has worshipped together in their home, singing and playing instruments, young and old lifting their voices to God.

Joining together in musical worship in your home will look many different ways, depending on what kind of musicians are under your roof. Start with a CD player and a variety of worship CDs, and encourage the whole family to sing right along with them. Play them loud enough to cover everybody's inhibitions and then just belt it out! Families with better musical abilities can be bolder in their arranging and orchestration. Remember, it doesn't have to be perfect, just from the heart.

I'm in awe of God's creativity in giving us music. It's all around us—in the sounds of nature,

Listen Together

Listening to music together is one of the most effective and creative methods of generating discussions about character, lifestyles, beliefs, creeds, and doctrines. No matter what song you hear, regardless of style or what it espouses, it is packed with thoughts and potential questions. Parents and their children or husbands and wives can never again say, "We don't have anything to talk about." Share a song and share your heart!

Setting Up Stones

in the laughter of our children, and flowing from the souls of musicians. I'm so thankful that this type of expression is available to us, enabling us to share with heaven's angels in the gift of singing praises to Almighty God. He loves it when we make music. He loves it when we drink deeply from the wells of worship and are caught up in melodies and harmonies that bring Him honor.

Favorite Song of All

He loves to hear the wind sing
As it whistles through the pines on mountain peaks
He loves to hear the raindrops
As they splash to the ground in a magic melody
He smiles in sweet approval
As the waves crash to the rocks in harmony
All creation joins in unity
To sing to Him majestic symphonies

(Chorus)
But His favorite song of all
Is the song of the redeemed
When lost sinners now made clean
Lift their voices loud and strong
When those purchased by His blood
Lift to Him a song of love
There's nothing more He'd rather hear
None so pleasing to His ear
As His favorite song of all

He loves to hear the angels
As they sing, "Holy, holy is the Lamb!"
Heaven's choirs in harmony
Lift up praises to the great I AM
But He lifts His hands for silence

When the weakest saved by grace begins to sing
And a million angels listen
As a newborn soul sings,
"I have been redeemed!"

That's His favorite song of all
The song of the redeemed
(Repeat rest of chorus)

(Bridge)
It's not just melodies and harmonies
That capture His attention
It's not just clever lines and phrases
That cause Him to stop and listen
But when any heart set free
Washed and bought by Calvary, begins to sing
(Repeat chorus)

Holy, holy, holy is the Lamb!
Hallelujah, Hallelujah!
Holy, holy, holy is the Lamb!
Hallelujah, Hallelujah!

Stone upon Stone

Do your personal tastes control what styles of music are listened to in your house?

How often do you listen to music together as a family? Do you discuss its impact, whether positive and negative?

Has your family ever heard you sing? Have you ever sung together as a family?

What are some ways you could begin to incorporate music, whether recorded or made by yourselves, into your home and worship times?

In what ways could you use other arts, like drama, writing, drawing, or painting, to allow your family members to express their love for God?

All Jesus did that day was tell stories—a long storytelling afternoon. His storytelling fulfilled the prophecy:
"I will open my mouth and tell stories;
I will bring out into the open things hidden since the world's first day."
—Matthew 13:34–35 (*The Message*)

8

It's Not Just a Story

Greg talks about some good times with a good friend, and how he learned to be a storyteller. The Singleton's son, Matt, emails them about *the* story. And Martha shares some ideas that really work to encourage open, creative discussion in your family.

Andraé Crouch is one of the most talented singers and songwriters in the history of Christian music. He was a pioneer, blazing a trail of contemporary worship that ushered in the phenomenal revival of the late 1960s and 1970s, known as the Jesus Movement. His music appears in virtually every hymnal published since that era, and his songs have been sung countless times throughout the world. Andraé now pastors New Christ Memorial Church in Southern California's San Fernando Valley. His pastoral ministry is vital and dynamic, and his thriving congregation is making a great impact on that community.

For almost 35 years, I have been blessed to call Andraé my friend. Christian music was beginning to seem stale to me back in the early 1970s when I was a teenager in a band playing in churches all around our area. When I discovered Andraé's music, combining a unique soulful sound and powerful message, I just had to get in touch with him. In a more uncomplicated era, his home phone number was easy to access, so I called him. We talked about God and music for the next two-and-a-half hours, and thus began a friendship that has lasted a lifetime. I've heard him sing thousands of songs and have sat in his church as he boldly and effectively proclaimed the Word of God.

Of his songs, "It's Not Just a Story" is one of my favorites.

I heard the story of Jesus,
Sounded like music in my ear.
Beautiful story of Jesus,
Dispelled my doubt and all my fear.
How marvelous is His love,
Brought to me from above.
And, oh, it's not just a story,
But reality.

Beautiful story of Jesus,
This world is longing to know.
Wonderful story of Jesus,
I'll take it wherever I go.
Tell of His love for this world,
To save every man, woman, boy and girl.
And, oh, it's not just a story,
Oh, it's not just a story,
Oh, that plain and simple story,
Became real to me.

As effective as every aspect of Andraé Crouch's ministry has been, as much acclaim as his music has received, what may be his greatest talent has been seen by relatively few people. Most of all, I love to sit face-to-face with him, across the table in a restaurant or in the living room, and hear him tell a story.

I've spent many evenings, almost till dawn, laughing until I thought I couldn't take any more, as he spun tale after tale from the events of his life. And the more I laugh, the more he laughs at me, and that spurs him on to relate still another adventure!

There's a unique aspect of Andraé's storytelling talent. In the midst of the chain of narratives, he can quickly change gears. A story that produces hilarious laughter might in the next moment remind him of a poignant truth, an evidence of God's faithfulness, or a dream that has been welling up inside of him. And suddenly, he will begin a moving and intimate

Setting Up Stones

account of his heavenly Father's work. And then we find ourselves quiet, sometimes even weeping. My heart is touched, and I am inspired.

We all know people like Andraé who are naturally good storytellers. They just seem to have a knack for communicating narratives that entertain, teach, or inspire. Their stories not only amuse us, but also, without a doubt, effectively convey important ideas and concepts.

Jesus was a storyteller. His stories resonated with His listeners. In His parables, Jesus fashioned truth into people's cultural frame of reference. He talked about fishing to fishermen, to teach His mission. He discussed the law with legal minds, to reveal His grace. He explained His Word to farmers in terms of agriculture. With businessmen, He revealed the significance of His salvation by explaining worth and value. There was nothing ethereal about the way Jesus explained things. He found common ground with the people He encountered and taught them truth drawing from everyday examples.

I've always wanted to be a great storyteller. I come from a long line of storytellers–generations who were the life of the party, holding the rapt attention of all those around them with tale after tale. Before my children were born, my best efforts, however, had always seemed only mildly entertaining. So when I finally came upon a willing

Once upon a Time

 The hardest part of telling a story is getting started. Try these icebreakers:

Ask family members to tell about a time when . . .
- God answered a prayer
- you were afraid
- God provided what you needed
- you *knew* God loved you
- God helped you through something really hard
- you did what was right
- you asked for forgiveness
- you forgave someone

One of our favorite things to do when our kids were smaller was what we call "story circle."

Someone starts by randomly choosing a character: "Once upon a time, there was a (little boy, turtle, toaster, flower, spider . . . whatever!) who lived in a (shoe, cereal box, mansion, etc.)." The first person gets the character and scene set. "One day, she was walking down the sidewalk, when_____ ."

Now, the first storyteller stops mid-sentence, and randomly points to another person, who picks up the story, and takes it anywhere he or she wants.

At some point, that person pauses, and points to another, who then picks up the tale.

The last person selected has to end the action, tie up the loose ends, and finish with, "And they lived happily ever after."

Sometimes, we did it just for fun, but it can work, too, if a parent starts the story with a biblical theme or a spiritual or moral conflict to be resolved.

Board Game Bonanza

Throughout the years, there have been a number of board games designed to encourage storytelling and the sharing of thoughts, dreams, and ideas. Many of them are appropriate for all ages, making them ideal when you get an urge to put together a family game night. Check the box descriptions for the age recommendations, and then make an investment that could bring plenty of fun into family times and will shed some great insights into everyone around the table.

Talicor/Aristoplay, Inc., is a game manufacturer that continues to make some great strides in this area and has consistently produced quality games of this type. The UnGame is probably their most successful. It's available in several versions, including a Christian version and pocket versions for times when you're stuck in traffic with a car full of cranky kids, and you need to have an alternative diversion for everybody! LifeStories, also a Talicor product, is another game that was popular in our house in the 1980s. All of these games, and many more are available at their Web site, www.aristoplay.com.

audience who hung onto every word of my narratives–my own two little ones, I was ready to hone my skills.

It was at the bedside of my five-year-old son that I learned how to tell a story. When he was younger and had used the inevitable tell-me-a-bedtime-story delay tactics, I had been more than willing to call on Mom to take over. But, at age five, when Matt looked up at me, and specifically requested that I participate, I had enough reason to give storytelling another try. He loved sports, still does, and so do I. So that seemed like a good starting place. As I sat at the side of his bed, I tentatively began to invent a character—a football player who looked amazingly similar to Matt. I recall the first story as being somewhat akin to ESPN *SportsCenter* highlights. But it clicked with my son! With Matt's enthusiastic encouragement, the next night brought more play-by-play. After a few evenings, I began to become more comfortable, and the stories began to be more multidimensional. Our fictional character began to face life decisions beyond the gridiron, giving me opportunity to address the inevitable situations that confront a young person growing up.

The stories took on a life of their own, and as I sat each evening at Matt's bedside, he began to add his own adventures for our fictional hero. Football season melded into basketball season, the sport and venue changed, and our star athlete faced even more situations that needed our input. Not only I, but Matt too, had become a storyteller. And those evenings that started so simply and hesitantly carried on for several years. We had so much fun, and important lessons were learned and values were instilled.

Stories are the most effective way to communicate God's truth in your home. It's not a new phenomenon. In fact, God Himself endorses it in His Word:

"Place these words on your hearts. Get them deep inside you. Tie them on your hands and foreheads as a reminder. Teach them to your children. Talk about

them wherever you are, sitting at home or walking in the street; talk about them from the time you get up in the morning until you fall into bed at night."
—Deuteronomy 11:18–19 (*The Message*)

This isn't a description of a classroom setting where the teacher presents a list of procedures and regulations. It certainly doesn't sound like a formal presentation of house rules and the do's and don'ts that all kids dread. Deuteronomy 11 is all about creating open lines of communication within our families. It's about talking things over. It's telling stories of what we have experienced and what we've heard. It's listening to our kids' stories without judgment or correction. It's a conversation, laced with observations of truth, ideas about life, and experiences with God.

In the movie *What About Bob?* (PG), starring Richard Dreyfuss as a psychiatrist and Bill Murray as Bob, his exceedingly neurotic patient, the good doctor has a simple but explicit prescription for his troubled patient: "baby steps." All of Bob's phobias can be cured if he will dare to take one little step at a time. Maybe your self-diagnosis is that you don't think you have it in you to become a storyteller. I can recall that, in my experience, it all began with me muddling through, making awkward attempts at being a storyteller. I want to share with you the same advice Bob's psychiatrist shared with him: baby steps. You have to start somewhere, and then, before you know it, you'll find your creativity beginning to flow and your comfort level will be on the rise.

Online Resource

The National Storytelling Network is a nonprofit organization for the advancement of storytelling. They host national contests, publish a magazine, and offer a wealth of information at the Web site, www.storynet.org.

In basketball, there are some players who are sometimes labeled "gym rats." These are players who lack the size or athleticism of their peers, but because they spend endless hours practicing their skills, they become effective on the court. Their nickname is derived from the fact that when everybody else goes home, they stay in the gym, still working with only the rats as an audience. It's not a pleasant thought, but it does make a point.

When it comes to storytelling, you're more than likely similar to me. Like the short gym rat who is slow and can't jump, we're not blessed with a lot of natural ability. Those gifted with innate talent are rare. But, knowing the value of stories to communicate truth and experience to our families should give us incentive to hone our skills. Practice, combined with the tenacity of our buddy the gym rat, can make anyone an effective storyteller. I'd like to share a few important principles to guide you as you make your initial attempts.

You have to know stories to tell stories. It all starts when you have a story to tell. Your local Christian bookstore has a treasure chest of children's books that you can begin reading your little ones. You can also check out your local public library. As you read these books

Time to Read

Building a personal library for each of your kids is important, but selecting books to be read together as a whole family opens up another dimension in reading. Stories rarely stand alone. The idea here is to read aloud to your family and then discuss together what you just read. A family reading time addresses some key issues in both your child's education and their spiritual development. It encourages a love for reading and provides a foundation for language skills. But family reading also creates an opportunity for you to have input regarding God and His truth, and allows you access into your child's own thoughts and understanding. As this reading time develops, allow other family members to be the designated reader for an evening. A wide selection of reading material will allow you to include everyone's interests, and the book doesn't necessarily have to be a Christian book, since you're there to discuss its theme, too. Here are some books that we found that might help get you started:

Hermie & Friends Series and Punchinello Series by Max Lucado (ages 3-8)
One of today's most prolific Christian authors offers this extended series of excellent books that target preschoolers and younger elementary school kids. There is such depth in the Christian themes, though, that it would be great for any age group to discuss them.

History Maker Biographies (ages 7-12)
This large selection of biographies (dozens are available) is marketed by Barnes & Noble Booksellers. They encourage discussion of character and perseverance.

Miracle on 49th Street, Hot Hand, The Big Field, Summer Ball, and Two-Minute Drill, by Mike Lupica (ages 12 and up)
Delicate life issues are addressed honestly by one of America's finest sportswriters in these teen novels. Some mature language and situations appear, but generally the conclusions offered are positive.

(continued)

to your children, try to pick up on the things they try to teach in high school literature classes—symbolism, metaphors, allegories, foreshadowing, and all the other things that make stories enjoyable. Don't you wish, now, that you'd paid more attention in Literature 101? I know a guy who actually got his degree in storytelling. You don't need to tackle another degree, though. There are plenty of books available on storytelling and creative communication at your local bookstore or library that will provide all the information you need.

The effort you invest in learning what makes a good story will act as a springboard to making you a more effective storyteller.

You have to know your story to tell stories. In order to weave stories that convey what is meaningful to you and important for your family, you have to determine just what your story is.

Martha has been teaching high school journalism a very long time. Please don't tell her I said that, because she's somewhat sensitive about it. One thing amazes me about her teaching, though. She is still able to communicate with her students as well now as she did years ago when she was only a few years older than they were. I know her secret. She has a collection of stories about her life that she shares with kids, and they love to hear them. Some of them are funny, some are kind of scary, and some are just simply heart wrenching. There are a few that are downright embarrassing, especially the ones where I play a role. But her students love them all. These stories not only capture her students' attention, Martha also uses them to illustrate both lessons in journalism and lessons in life. And probably most significant of all, her storytelling creates an atmosphere of joy and openness in her classroom, and builds a solid connection with those students that lasts long past their high school days.

Every year, former students make pilgrimages back to the journalism room at their alma mater to see her. Some of them are just finishing their first year of college; some are grown and have high school-age children of their own. She gives the alumni a tour of the facilities to show them how things have changed and introduces every one of them to the current students as "one of my all-time favorites." Then, inevitably, the returnee says, "Ms. Sing, have you told them the story about the time you . . ."

Time to Read

Family Faith Treasury: A Year of Inspirational Stories, edited by Eva Moore (ages 4-12)
This collection of Bible stories and classics is a perfect conversation starter.

Hank the Cowdog Series, by John Erickson (ages 8-12)
Maybe this extensive series was one of our family's favorites because it's all about Texas and ranching, but even non-Texans will discover that these books are creative and entertaining for everyone. Our son, Matt, after earning his master's degree in reading and literacy, moved back to San Antonio to begin teaching. One of his first orders of business was to get a library card. He was shocked not only to find that his old card was still active, but that he owed a 12-year-old late fee on a Hank the Cowdog book.

The American Girls Collection (ages 8-12)
From a female perspective, kids learn American history, and the books' themes encourage discussions that lead to positive decisions.

The Big Book of What, How, and Why, by Bob Strauss (ages 8-12)
These are bedtime stories for all the analytical, left-brained kids! If your family is into science and technology, read one of these amazing offerings and then discuss what a big God we serve.

God's Wisdom for Little Girls, by Elizabeth George, and *God's Wisdom for Little Boys,* by Jim and Elizabeth George (both for ages 4-8)
The Georges have written these beautiful books that present the attributes of godly character taught in Proverbs.

What is it about our personal stories that makes them so attractive? It could be that stories act as a door that opens to allow our children to see who we really are. And then, they understand that we really *can* identify with them. We create a connection there. So then, when it comes to conversations with them about the things of God, they instinctively know that we won't be shocked or judgmental when they have questions. They'll know that we're on a journey with God, just like they are.

When you start telling your stories, it's all about research and rehearsal. Write a narrative that details events in your life. Recollections of single significant events in your life are more effective than a chronology that drones on ("Then I did this, and then I did that..."). It doesn't matter whether they are funny or sad, just that you include as many details as possible. Tell all about where you were, what you heard, how you felt, and what you thought about. Above all, this is not a time to preach!

Do you want to be even more adventurous? Research your family tree and interview relatives about the lives of ancestors. Then, tell their stories too.

You have to know God's story to tell stories. The foundation of all the stories that you tell should be the values and truths that God teaches us through His Word and His work in our lives. Some of the most exciting adventures you'll ever find are the stories of men and women in the Bible. And just as significant to your children are the stories of God's faithfulness to your family through the years.

The Classics

There are plenty of "children's versions" of classic literature that have been simplified for beginning readers, but there's something very special about gathering the entire family close around you and experiencing together the original, rich language and vivid images evoked by a great story that leaves a lasting impression.

In addition to reading all seven of C. S. Lewis's *The Chronicles of Narnia*, which we highly recommend, a visit to the children's classics section of your local bookstore or library will give you so many good reading options you may find your kids are grown before you can share them all.

Books like *Swiss Family Robinson* (Johann D. Wyss), *Treasure Island* (Robert Louis Stevenson), *Little Women* (Louisa May Alcott), *Old Yeller* (Fred Gipson), *Black Beauty* (Anna Sewell), *Gulliver's Travels* (Jonathan Swift), or the *Little House on the Prairie* (Laura Ingalls Wilder) series open up hours of delight, and when talked over, create great windows of opportunity for building faith and values in your children's hearts and minds.

God's story is ongoing, from the beginning of time throughout history, and through the lives of every person who has walked the face of the earth. Our goal is to show our children how real God's story is, and how meaningful He is to our lives and theirs right now.

A few years back, after the premier showing of Mel Gibson's movie *The Passion of the Christ*, I received an email from my son, Matt, who was away at college. His insights express my thinking well. Here are some excerpts from that email:

Dad,

Tonight, I went with some friends from church . . . to the premier of *The Passion of the Christ* . . . . The film was superbly done . . . . It was symbolic, artistic, cutting edge. It met all the qualities of a plain-old great movie, but that's not what I leave thinking about.

Thank God. It's the story itself that was moving to hear again. Though seeing it put onto the big screen in a realistic, powerful, and well-done way was a good thing, I also realized that the fact that it was on film didn't affect the story one bit. Thank God that He doesn't need a movie to make His story more meaningful . . . . The story is what made the film transcendent, and not the film that made the story transcendent . . .

I was afraid that I "needed" the story of my Christ to be in a well-done movie for me to really understand it; but thank God, His story is even bigger than the greatest movie! I found myself gazing up at the ceiling of the theatre at one point, and I remember thinking, "Wow, this is great, but the story represented here is bigger than even this . . . it is outside of the theatre, it is off the screen, it is huge . . . this is the story here on this screen, and it is a beautiful and horrid depiction . . . but the story is bigger still!"

I left there resonating with a story that resonates in me. This is my story. This is my song. It is real. The movie didn't make it any more or less real than what it is in me, to me. Thank God that though He uses many people and many things to tell His story, He needs none and nothing to give the story any iota of added merit . . . .

Hear God's story more, look for it more. Read it, seek it, live it. It is alive. It is not fully contained on any film, scroll, thin gold-lined paper, song, artistic masterpiece, human word or deed. It is much bigger, much more alive than any of these things . . . .

Thank God that even in our best efforts, even in our finest films, even our greatest artists, even in our best words, we cannot contain Him! This is something to remember.

Love, Matt

I can't say that when I sat at Matt's bedside years ago and shared stories with him, I knew for sure that he would grasp what the real story, God's story, was all about. Somehow, he mulled over all the scenarios, the ideas, and the truths in our bedtime stories, and the Holy Spirit caused something to spring up within him. Thank God.

I'm not certain how it happened. But I can say this: the most fulfilling aspect of my life has been seeing the story—the good news of Jesus and His work in the world—come alive in my children. I do know for certain that something meaningful was communicated to them during those simple story times.

- Stories—fantasies, novels, and various fiction—imparted principles and truths to build on.
- Stories of events from my own childhood formed connections that created bonds.
- Stories of our family's faith over generations crafted identity.
- Stories of God's love and faithfulness developed assurance in Him.

"Tell me a story, Daddy," takes on a new significance in light of all this. We need to seize every moment and every occasion that we can to reveal to our children the reality of God and the relevance of Jesus's redeeming work in our lives. Let's develop the creativity God has given each of us and share with our children the stories of our life, our faith, and our God.

Stone upon Stone

What events in your life history would make a good story? From elementary school? From high school? From college? How you and your spouse met? When the kids were born?

What "rescue" stories from your walk with God can you tell your family?

When has God answered your family's prayers or met your needs in an amazing way?

Have you ever specifically asked your parents, your grandparents, or your children to tell you their stories?

How could sharing stories like this lead your family into deeper worship?

So here's what I want you to do, God helping you: Take your everyday, ordinary life—your sleeping, eating, going-to-work, and walking-around life—and place it before God as an offering.
—Romans 12:1 (*The Message*)

Building Altars

Martha shares some stories that reveal how, for generations, spiritual foundations were formed in her family and Greg's family. She offers some practical ways to create the same atmosphere in today's homes, including writing a family creed. She then tells the story of the Passover celebration and her first chance to experience it firsthand.

Altars are places of remembrance, places of commitment, and places of sacrifice. Lessons are learned and directions are determined at altars. Joshua didn't haphazardly pile up stones to create an altar. God had instructed him as to the purpose of the stones, and that they were to be arranged so that they conveyed a message. He purposefully set up the stones in a way that they would not be easily disturbed. In our homes, the "stones" that we use are our beliefs, experiences, principles, and strategies, from which we build altars that are not easily shaken. We use all these stones purposefully to create the ideals that define who we are as a family. We're building altars. These altars, then, become foundational to establishing our home as a place of true worship.

If we would build an altar for our families, then we must spend some time and prayerful thought in choosing our stones and designing their arrangement. Just as Joshua experienced, we can't expect our altar of stone to just happen. We must begin by deciding who we will be as a family and exactly how we will go about our business of worshipping God.

Our Heritage

As I grew up, my family's identity and mission were conveyed to me in moments of instruction, or in little stories, as moments randomly occurred. The same was true of Greg. From earliest remembrance, I can still hear my parents' voices telling me: "We don't lie;" "We don't hit people;" "We don't eat without washing our hands." There were also some "We-don't-wear-white-shoes-before-Easter" and "We-don't-shake-hands-with-our-gloves-on" statements, but those are for another story! The point is, I absorbed a moral and spiritual family code from my parents' instructions, which were engraved on my heart and mind as a part of my identity from my earliest days.

For Greg, too, there was a sense of spiritual identity passed along in the form of often-repeated stories. Greg's dad, C. B., grew up during the Depression, living on a farm with eight sisters and a brother. His family history is full of tales of love and laughter and God's practical provision.

When C. B. was about ten years old, the only pants he owned developed a hole so large that he would no longer be able to attend school until he could get a new pair. There was no money for a new pair of pants right away, and besides that, it wasn't even his turn to get new pants. So he was going to have to wait until enough egg money could be set aside for the unexpected purchase.

"I was walking down the dirt road from our farm to town," C. B. would tell us, "and as I was walking, I was praying, 'Lord, you know I really need a pair of pants, but Mama and Papa just can't buy one right now.' And then, my eye fell on something shiny over in the ditch along side the road.

"I went over and picked it up, and it was a quarter! So, I went on into town, and went to the store to see about a pair of pants. I prayed all the way to town, and when I got there, I found me a pair that cost exactly 25 cents!" he would exclaim.

Our children love that story, and every time Pa told it, it served as an altar where once again we could all remember that God has been forever faithful to supply every need as our family looks to and trusts Him.

The Singleton Family Creed

For every parent, there's plenty of angst and apprehension when those little ones reach the age where they begin to wander from the nest to mingle with the big world. As we sought to prepare our children to play in the neighborhood, to participate in organized sports, and to attend public school, we wanted above all for them to understand their own identities, not only as our children and a part of our family, but as children of their heavenly Father.

We talked often about how not every mommy and daddy know about Jesus, and not every friend the children meet would, either.

"There are times when you will just be different," we told them, "because you belong to

Jesus." We talked about issues that might come up, from witches and ghosts at Halloween, to what was on TV, to seeing others being mistreated, and we talked about what Jesus would want them to do in those situations.

Just as Joshua and the Israelites with him arranged the stones as an altar so that others would see, our altar is what others see about our families. Our altars stand as an encouragement to other families of believers and serve as a testimony to unbelievers who come into our lives and homes. They should be crafted carefully, and purposefully, to be a mission statement for our homes.

As our children progressed through elementary school, we were filled with joy to observe that they saw themselves as missionaries to both the children and the adults around them. When Annie's second-grade teacher told the class that she had miscarried her baby, Annie went up, put her arms around her, and prayed for her. As a fifth grader, Matt stood, with only the school custodian and a handful of other children, and led prayer on the first official See You at the Pole day. They each found opportunity to share the story of Jesus and lead others to faith in Him during recess on a number of occasions.

As they approached middle school, we determined the need to place another stone on our altar of family worship, to reinforce and strengthen the foundation we had already laid. The inspiration came from an unexpected source. Mike Singletary was one of the most intimidating linebackers in pro football history. He led the Chicago Bears to a Super Bowl championship in 1986, and he's a member of the Pro Football Hall of Fame. I was especially fond of him, because he is a fellow alumnus of Baylor University. He won Greg's football-loving heart when we saw him play his freshman year at Baylor. That day, he tackled an Air Force Academy Falcon ball carrier so hard that it cracked his helmet, the first of 16 times that that happened while Mike was in college.

Mike Singletary is a wonderful man of God and a dynamic communicator. We heard him speaking about his family once, and he mentioned that they had written a family creed to establish who they were and what they believed as a family. The creed is responsible for providing the foundation of faith and character in their home. What an awesome way to set up stones for their family!

We saw the value of building this altar for our family, too. So, we took a weekend away, for the specific purpose of praying and searching Scripture, and writing a family creed.

As the weekend came to a close, we spent several hours around the table in our motel room, with all four of us working together, giving ideas and input on the exact wording, carefully crafting our "Singleton Family Creed." (See sidebar, "A Family Creed.")

Once home, we printed it, framed it, and gave it a place of prominence in our living room.

Through their teen years, our kids brought a constant stream of friends through our house. Some were church friends and fellow believers, but many others were lost, hurt, and seeking. Our children brought them to our altar—our home—as a place where they, too, might find mercy, grace, and peace.

That family creed served as an altar that reminded them of their identity and mission as they charted the often dangerous waters of their teen years. Instead of being intimidated by the world, they each reached out, because they understand themselves in light of the altar of our home.

Learning from the Master

Stone upon stone, we build our family altar from lessons, large and small, that teach us what it means to belong to God and to worship Him with all of our might. And, master teacher that He is, God has not left us to figure out how to do this on our own.

The Old Testament is filled with God's instructions for feasting and fasting, for setting up altars. It always fascinates me when an Old Testament scholar teaches on such a passage, unlocking the culture of the day to reveal symbols that the people at the time would have understood, but that we today may not be aware of. Once revealed, though, these symbols can in turn help us see more wonderful truths about our Father.

A survey of Jesus's teaching in the Gospels reveals that He used the same method— taking an object or a common activity and using it to illustrate the lesson He was teaching. A water pot at a wedding, a coin in the mouth of a fish, a mustard seed, an olive tree—all of these became props, or symbols, that the Master Teacher used to capture the attention of His followers.

For instance, returning to the Old Testament, God intended a ceremonial meal, the Passover, to help the Israelites define who they are as a people and who they are in relation to Him. We can learn at least three specific steps to effective teaching both from the explicit commands regarding Passover in Scripture (Exodus 12) and its traditional observance by Jewish families (the *Haggadah*, based on but not entirely found in Scripture).

First, God used something concrete, but out of the ordinary, to capture their attention. The Passover in one sense is just an ordinary meal, but in another sense it is completely different from other meals. The traditional Passover *Haggadah*, or "order of service," calls for the youngest son to repeat the question over and over, "Why is this night different from all other nights?" As you read the ceremony, you discover that the food is different, the table setting is different, the order in which food is eaten is different. It even calls for a stranger, someone who is not normally at the table, to be present.

The child's question prompts the father to explain the symbolism of each food, of the empty chair, of the three pieces of matzo, which in turn leads everyone to reflect on what God did when He brought Israel out of slavery in Egypt. Just as He did later with Joshua—having them put stones in their living rooms—God gave the families something tangible, but unusual, to stir their curiosity and prompt questions. It is important to notice, too, that the Passover

Take Action!

In Scripture, we see many occasions where God directed His children to a specific activity that would serve as an object lesson and would serve as a timely altar in their lives. We can often effectively adapt these activities to serve the same purpose in our homes.

As a way to emphasize humility and service to one another as components of family worship, wash one another's feet. Provide historical context by letting the kids know that, in Jesus's day, travel was on foot, on the same roads that animals traveled, so people's feet were tired and truly filthy. Washing a person's feet was not a pleasant task. You can kneel, remove the family member's shoes, dip their feet in a basin of water, and then dry them with a towel. As you do, express out loud your love and commitment to that person.

When one member, or the family as a whole, faces a particularly difficult challenge, have a "Jericho march." Walk single file around the perimeter of the place that symbolizes the challenge, with each member praying silently on points you have agreed on ahead of time. Once everyone is back in the car, you can shout together, "Hallelujah! Amen!", which means, "God be praised! Establish it!" (See Chapter 10 for more on the Jericho march).

In much the same manner that some Jewish households celebrate Sabbath, set the table with a cloth and candles, and gather the family. Light the candles and sing a worship chorus or hymn. Dad leads the family in Communion, perhaps with each family member speaking a simple sentence of thanks or praise before drinking the cup.

For younger children, spend a weekend night acting out a favorite Bible story. Assign parts and improvise costumes and props. Or, for older kids, translate a Bible story to a modern-day setting. Videotape it, then have fun watching yourselves on television. Talk about what God is teaching in the story.

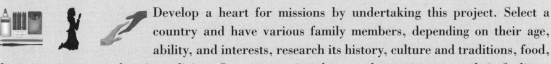

Develop a heart for missions by undertaking this project. Select a country and have various family members, depending on their age, ability, and interests, research its history, culture and traditions, food, dress, music, art, and major religion. On a set evening, have each person present their findings, along with pictures, maps, and other illustrations. Go all out, and prepare the food, play the music, and make the event feel special. A trip to the dollar store might yield props, costume pieces, and other essential items. Make it fun! Spend the next month praying daily for the people of that country and the missionaries who serve them. If possible, contact missionaries in your researched country (or one nearby) through your church. Find out how you can help them and pray for them. Send a care package. You can also expand this idea by choosing a state or city other than your own to research and lift up in prayer.

Haggadah has a part for everyone to play—the eldest son or daughter, the youngest child, the mother, and even the stranger.

From this first step so to speak, we learn that the most effective activities we plan for our families may start with a seemingly ordinary object or an activity that is just out of the ordinary enough to capture their attention and cause them to ask questions. This is a practice that I have seen work over and over in my classroom. Even the most sophisticated senior honors student who enters my class and sees anything out of the ordinary, whether it is colored tape marking off a square on the floor, a string of plastic garage sale signs hanging from the ceiling, or a line of front pages from other schools' newspapers hanging on the bulletin board, will stop short, and say, "What's this for? What are we going to do?" I have hooked them into the day's lesson by arousing their curiosity.

We want, as well, to plan a way for every person to participate and become more than spectators. In the Passover *Haggadah*, the oldest children actually have speaking parts, while the youngest are asked to find the hidden bread, allowing each member of the family to operate at their own level of intellect and skills. It is important when we are planning moments of family worship to think of ways to include each member of the family on the level at which they are able to function. We might ask a child in upper elementary school to read a Bible verse; a child in prekindergarten needs to be allowed to answer a question after a story, point to a detail in a picture, or sing a simple chorus. Teenagers need to be given more responsible roles, as well as some ownership in the whole process.

Second, as the families participate, and as their curiosity prompts questions, a connection is made between the activity and the truth it illustrates. Just as God explained to Joshua that the stones marked the two trips through the water over dry ground, God created a symbol of the blood of the Lamb of God—Jesus—foretold in the Passover as blood is placed on the doorposts in the sign of a cross, so that death would not touch those "covered" by the blood. In the Passover service, each element—the four cups of wine, the bitter herbs, the egg, the broken matzo—is explained for what it represents from that first Passover in Egypt. We can do the same in our homes, through question and answer, discussion, and explanation that leads our household to think about the meaning behind an activity and respond.

Finally, God uses the moment He has created to teach principles that can be applied broadly in the whole context of their lives. From remembering the deliverance from Egypt in the Passover observance, to recognizing two different excursions through parted water on dry ground, the people learn that their God is a strong and faithful deliverer of His children. It is as we too recognize these lessons and begin to apply them in our lives that we move toward being a family of worshipers.

Before I married Greg, I shared an apartment with another teacher who was Jewish. Her family warmly welcomed me to their home on many occasions. At Passover, I was honored to be given the role of "stranger" and invited to participate in their observance.

A Family Creed

The focus of our second family retreat was defining ourselves as a Christian family, and discovering God's purpose for our family. At the end of the day, all of us discussed our family's identity and mission and wrote the following family creed, which is now framed and displayed in a prominent place in our home. This can serve as a guideline from which you can write your own.

Singleton Family Creed
Set forth on the 20th day of August in the year of our Lord, 1994.

We are the Singletons.

Recognizing God's hand on our family's life throughout many generations, we affirm our faith in the Almighty God; His Son, Jesus Christ, our Savior; and the sanctifying work of the Holy Spirit.

The foundation of our home is God's Holy Word. Our mission is to bring glory to God, and to minister to others, pointing them to God and His principles of living.

As individual members of the family, we pledge to lift each other daily in prayer, to support each other's endeavors, to strive for unity in our midst, to speak words of healing, encouragement and restoration to each other, and to stand shoulder to shoulder against Satan, the enemy of our souls.

We determine as individuals to honor our family name, and to do or say nothing that would bring reproach upon it, or upon our God. In all that we undertake, we pledge to work wholeheartedly, as unto God.

It is our earnest prayer that all generations that may follow us, until the coming of our Lord Jesus, will know the joy, fulfillment, and power to be found in serving God, reaching out to others, and loving each other.

As the service began, and I looked around the table at the family gathered there, I was overwhelmed at the idea that from this family in the Texas Panhandle to their grandparents in Russia to great-grandparents and ancestors reaching back in a direct line for thousands of years, they had kept this feast intact, year after year, in an unbroken line of fathers to sons since that first night in Egypt.

Now, having grown up in Sunday School (and having seen *The Ten Commandments* with Charlton Heston), I knew every detail of the story of God through Moses leading the children of Israel out of Egypt. I also knew every detail of Jesus's last supper with His disciples. And I knew there was a connection between the two.

But as I sat at the table with my friend's family, observing Passover in much the same manner that Jesus had, I began to understand the context in a way I never had, and Christ's words and actions took on a deeper meaning than ever before. When my friend's father took the middle piece of matzo (striped and pierced!) and snapped it in half, I could hear Jesus saying, "From now on, this is my body, broken for you." And when the family drank the last glass of wine, in hope of the coming of Messiah, I fully understood what Jesus was saying when He declared (my paraphrase), "This is the new promise of salvation, my blood, shed for you. From now on when you do this, do it in remembrance of me." (See Luke 22:17–20; 1 Corinthians 11:24–25.)

At the end of the evening, when my friend's father asked me what I had thought of their observance, I told him truly that because of it, I would never approach communion in the same way again.

For me, the three principles had worked exactly as they should. The observance captured my attention and stirred my curiosity and imagination. Then, I began to understand a deeper message and meaning behind it all. And finally, I came away from the experience with a deep, personal understanding that, 35 years later, still affects my approach to the communion table.

Twenty-First-Century Updates

So what would applying these principles look like in the twenty-first century home?

One particular morning, when Matt was in late elementary and Annie was in early middle school, Greg captured our attention by placing tiny, one-inch square boxes, perfectly wrapped in minute detail, at each of our plates at breakfast.

Of course the questions came: "Hey, what's this?" "Can I open it?"

Greg read Bible verses referring to God's gift of salvation and how God desires that we make a gift of our whole hearts to Him, thereby connecting those little boxes to the devotional theme for the day.

"Keep these boxes where you will see them," Greg told us, "and always let them remind you of the gift of salvation Jesus gave to us, and the gift of our hearts and lives that we can give to Him."

It was a very simple exercise. But, its effectiveness was illustrated recently, more than ten years later, when each of us, albeit sheepishly, produced our tiny boxes from our personal keeping places and admitted that we still use them as reminders today.

Have you ever gone through one of those empty times, spiritually? There's no significant crisis that you're facing, but you just feel as if you're simply adrift. We all experience seasons like that, but, once, we found our whole family seemingly bogged down there. We had no purpose or direction as a family, even though we all still loved God and none of us were rebelling and shaking our fist in His face. We were all just empty.

I don't believe we wandered into our neighborhood Christian bookstore with any intentions to turn the tide that day. A visit there was part of our routine, a time to see some friendly faces and enjoy some fellowship. But, on this particular day we found a book that created a spark for us.

Jack Hayford had written a book entitled *Glory on Your House*, and that title seemed as bright as a neon sign as it sat on the shelf that day. We were familiar with Pastor Hayford's dynamic ministry in southern California, and we were interested to see what insight he might have for our home.

We bought the book, came home, and started reading. In the book, Hayford describes a moment that took place many years ago at Church on the Way in Van Nuys, California. As he was praying one Saturday night with the three members of his pastoral staff, he sensed that God was asking something unusual of them. So, at Hayford's direction, the four separated, taking up positions at the corners of the sanctuary and extending their hands toward the middle of the room as though they were lifting a tent top. As they began with prayerful praise, God's presence seemed to fill the room.

Over the following weeks, Hayford came to see that night as symbolic of Revelation 4, where four living creatures stand at each corner of the throne of God and continually worship Him. The experience confirmed for him that the church's worship had brought the sanctuary into spiritual alignment with the throne of God. Hayford writes,

> It is a benefit available to anyone, anyplace, who will commit himself, or themselves, to having a "house" founded in worshiping the true and living God, and exalting His Son Jesus Christ. I saw that the four angelic beings had not taken their stations at our address; rather, our worship had aligned us with God's address!
> —Jack Hayford, *Glory on Your House*

The next morning, as our family finished breakfast, we each stood at a corner of the dining room table and started our day with a moment of worship together. That simple exercise became a daily occurrence for us, and we began, as a family, to experience a new unity of purpose. We stepped out into the world every day knowing that each one of us was committed to God's purposes and to His work in each of us. Daily building that altar in our home established direction, inspiration, and security for our entire family, simply by creating a concrete, symbolic picture of a spiritual reality.

God's principles are timeless and unchanging. Now, as in Joshua's day, for an altar of family worship to stand, we cannot rely on assumptions or leave it to chance. Each of our families is unique, and we each will find in God unique direction for determining what the altars in our homes will be and how we carefully and purposefully can arrange the stones that will become those places of remembrance, commitment, and sacrifice.

Stone upon Stone

What activities do each member of your family enjoy? What activities do you all enjoy together as a family? How could you adapt some of these to focus on God?

What talents or abilities have you observed in each member of the family? How can you create opportunities for them use those as an offering of worship in your home?

If you were to write a family creed, what would you include in it? Who are you as a family? What do you want to become? What principles do you live by?

"This is a day you are to commemorate; for the generations to come you shall celebrate it as a festival to the LORD —a lasting ordinance."
—Exodus 12:14

10

Traditions Become Treasures

Traditions have always been important to God's people, and Martha discusses what a family needs to do to build them in their home. She also recalls the time the wise men got lost on their way to the manger. And how about some ideas that call for celebrations every month of the year?

God has always had plans for His people.

The children of Israel weren't special to Him because they were mightier than any other nation, but simply because they belonged to Him. Not long after He crafted the Ten Commandments, God made a promise to His people, which is chronicled in Deuteronomy 7. He told them that they were to be different than other people. His plan was that their goals would be different, their attitudes would be different, and their actions would be different. Because He had delivered them from a life of slavery, they were now free to enter into this covenant with Him. He promised that if they acknowledged Him as the only true God and kept the Commandments His love, protection, and blessing would be theirs for a thousand generations. He sealed their agreement by establishing traditions, feasts, and holy days for them, to demonstrate that covenant of love.

For thousands of years, devout Jews have faithfully observed these feast days and have practiced the traditions that God designed for them. In this way, they have preserved their unique identity as His chosen people, though they have been repeatedly scattered and nearly obliterated. A spiritual legacy has been passed unbroken from generation to generation.

Goals in Designing Traditions

As you seek to develop traditions that will make a lasting spiritual impact on your children, keep in mind these objectives. Does the tradition help your family

- hide God's Word in your hearts using activities that illustrate biblical truths?
- remember specific blessings that God has given to your family?
- encourage everyone's participation in thanking Him?
- affirm each family member's standing with God and with the rest of the family?
- establish a unique identity?
- create a legacy or heritage of faith?
- rejoice, have fun, be glad?

As surely today as in the days of Moses, God seeks to show us who He is and who we are in Him, that He may bless us and also those who follow us. Traditions, feasts and celebrations are still an effective way to bring our families closer to God, day by day and generation to generation. In the pattern of Passover, we have seen how God designed a tangible activity to illustrate an intangible, but eternally important, lesson regarding His mercy and saving grace through the blood of Jesus Christ. Similarly, we can bring our families to consider God and His ways, passing on our faith and values, in the midst of our holidays and milestones as well as in everyday life. We can develop spiritual traditions of our own, each of which can become a stone in the altar of our family worship. But remember, to be effective, traditions must always be evolving, or else, over time, they can become boring, then meaningless, or even legalistic.

Plastic Nativity to Lasting Tradition

The first Christmas that we were married, we purchased a lovely ceramic nativity set that we thought would be the focus of our decorations for years to come. But we were not thinking like parents!

Then came the kids...who were fascinated by the figures, and whose little hands just itched to play with baby Jesus. Greg pointed out that "No, no!" was not really a message we wanted to give our toddlers in relation to anything having to do with Jesus, so we bought a really cheap, really lurid plastic set for the kids to handle all they wanted. Granted, the red for Mary's mouth was actually somewhere under her ear, and the pupils of Joseph's eyes were level with the end of his nose, but those details never seemed to bother our children.

One year, we used the set to let the kids act out the Christmas story as Greg read it from the Bible, a small portion of the story being read each night through December. They started with an empty stable under the coffee table, Mary and Joseph in our bedroom, the wise men in Annie's bedroom, and the shepherds in the dining room. Each night, as another part of the story unfolded, Annie and Matt would run to move the characters a little closer to Bethlehem.

Everyone participated; everyone was engaged.

I took baby Jesus, and wrapped the figure in the most beautiful, most intriguing package under the tree. By Christmas Eve, all the six–inch figures were at or near the stable, but the manger was empty.

On Christmas morning, that package was in the stable, with a tag that read, "To the whole world, with love, from God." We opened the package, put baby Jesus in the manger, and had a family worship and communion time.

This struck such a chord with our children that they wanted to repeat it the next year, and the next, and so a tradition of family worship for the Christmas season was born. Of course, there was the year that the wise men were missing in action for over a week, until Greg discovered them in the heater closet when he went to change the filter. Despite that mishap, we all count our Christmas morning worship time as the highlight of the season.

Worship in All Seasons

These few ideas will get you jump-started on establishing traditions that direct your family to worship through the seasons of the year. You should add your own touches, and adapt them to your family's individual personality and interests. No matter how you do it, be assured that the effort to establish your own spiritual traditions will certainly result in some treasured moments of family unity in the presence of God.

New Year: On January 1, meet as a family to prayerfully set a spiritual goal or select a key verse for the year. At midnight on the following December 31, review the year in light of your goal or verse and give thanks and celebrate God's faithfulness to you in that year.

Valentine's Day: Begin thinking and discussing on February 1 what your family could do as a Valentine for Jesus—a special offering, an outreach, or service project in which everyone participates, and so forth.

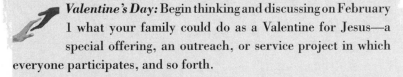

St. Patrick's Day: Yes, on this day we all are Irish...but this is a good time to look at old photos, tell some family stories, and celebrate your heritage of faith. If your family is the first generation of believers, talk about the legacy of faith you want to establish, and list things you can do from day to day to make that happen. Make it fun with decorations, a favorite family food for dinner, and a general celebration of your cultural roots!

(continued on page 120)

As the kids have grown, we have adjusted the depth of the devotions and the level of their participation accordingly, but we have maintained the basic tradition. When Annie and Matt reached high school, we decided that each family member would take one Christmas figure and study and meditate on the Scriptures related to that character. Then we all shared what we learned in the family devotion time. How precious it was to listen to our teenagers effectively share from the Word and lead *us* in family devotions!

Given the importance teenagers place on being cool, you might think that they would begin to find such traditions corny or somehow too old-school. But with 36 years of experience as adviser to high school yearbook staffs, I have learned that teenagers love traditions and become agitated at the thought of anyone changing them.

Worship in All Seasons

Easter: Because Easter Sunday for us has generally been spent with extended family and in-laws going in every direction for food, games, and an egg hunt, we wanted to adopt a seasonal tradition for our own household that involved a special time of worship. And, for that reason, we began our Passover celebration.

We found a copy of the Passover *Haggadah* that had added Christian applications, and we began to celebrate Passover in our home. Our kids were immediately captivated by the ceremony and the symbolic foods (although, for some inexplicable reason, Matt *liked* the bitter herbs, and wanted more!), and they fulfilled their roles with a solemn sense of importance.

While most churches have a full slate of worship services and activities for this season, it is still important to set a spiritual tradition for your own family. Observing Passover seems like a natural, but you could hold your own sunrise service, or have a Good Friday family communion time, where family members share what Jesus's crucifixion and resurrection means to them personally.

(continued)

Not only do my students become almost militant at the idea of changing the way we've always done it, they also quickly latch onto things as traditions. It only takes doing the same thing twice in the same way for them to add it to the lexicon. I cannot tell you how many high school seniors I have heard grumble in a much-aggrieved manner because their moms chose to buy new ornaments for the Christmas tree or talked of turning their bedroom into an exercise or sewing room!

I have come to believe that this reaction occurs because tradition gives them a sense of security. At a time in their lives when changes are rapid and ongoing and when they must find the courage to venture out on their own, traditions remind them who they are and where they come from and assure them that some important things will not change.

Even after our children graduated from college and beyond, the tradition still remained fresh and meaningful to our family. Months before her wedding, our daughter called to tell us that her fiancé would be with us for Thanksgiving. She asked if we could begin the nativity pilgrimage and devotion time while he was with us. They eagerly began to share this spiritual tradition after they were married, and now they look forward to establishing new traditions of family worship in their own home.

Jericho March Marks a Milestone

Just before Annie, our daughter, entered first grade, her first year in public school, we looked for a symbolic, dramatic way to prepare her for what lay ahead. A family milestone like this not only needed to be observed, but we wanted to use it to allay any fears Annie might have about this next big step in her life. We turned once again to the Bible and found a vivid symbol of what we wanted to accomplish.

We felt the story of Joshua and the battle of Jericho illustrated some of the challenges that we would face in the public school system. Here's the context: The Israelites were finally ready to enter their place of promise. It represented to them a bright future, but there were obstacles that needed to be dealt with head on. Jericho was a Canaanite stronghold, and in order for the Hebrews to attain all that God had for them, they would have to conquer that city. Maybe Joshua had in mind that they should achieve the victory militarily, with his own strategies and display of strength. If they stormed the gates, with slashing swords and bold aggression, his army could perhaps take Jericho, forcing it into submission.

But God had another idea. He directed the people to march silently around the city once a day for six days. Then they marched around Jericho seven times on the seventh day. Finally, with trumpets blasting and shouts of victory, God delivered the city to them. As the walls fell, they were able to walk into the city unimpeded and conquer it. Through

Worship in All Seasons

  Fiesta! This is a San Antonio thing, we know . . . but it is a huge, wonderful, weeklong block party and celebration with food, music, parades, parties, queens in lovely dresses, and a king. Sort of like heaven, with a Latin flavor! At some point in the year, for no other reason than that He is worthy, just **celebrate**! Decorate, feast, play joyful praise music, and recount to each other the joys of being children of the king!

 Fourth of July: At some time amidst the hot dogs and fireworks, gather as a family to thank God for the freedom we have to praise Him, to speak of Him. Then talk about and pray for those in other countries who, even now, are being imprisoned, tortured, or put to death for their faith. Research the persecuted church online. Ask God to make you good stewards of your freedom!

   Halloween: On October 31, as a family look for a way to counteract the devilishness. Walk your neighborhood, silently praying for your neighbors, or pass out candy with a simple Bible verse attached. And talk to your children about how the whole Halloween deal is actually a rip-off of November 1, All Saints Day. On that day, have a Bible character costume party, relate the stories of Bible heroes, or read a story about a hero of the faith from a later century. For older children, read an entry from *Foxe's Book of Martyrs*, a classic book that chronicles the stories of Christians who gave their lives for their faith.

(continued on page 122)

Worship in All Seasons

Thanksgiving: One way to celebrate Thanksgiving begins with each person having just a few kernels of corn on his or her dinner plate, to commemorate those first difficult months when the colonists had so little to eat. After eating those, give thanks for God's bountiful blessing, and began the feast. Why not adopt this tradition, which reminds us of the abundance of God's goodness? Or, go around the table with each person offering a sentence prayer thanking God for something for which they are, especially thankful.

Christmas: Particularly in the United States, this is the season of the year most filled with tradition. It is a joyful, exciting time for many families. But be sure that you focus on worshipping God. A really wonderful idea is for the family to spend time, effort, and resources each year planning, preparing, and presenting a birthday gift to Jesus. This could be a sacrificial offering, volunteering as a family, or perhaps a secret mission of anonymously helping someone needy, sick, homeless, or alone...in Jesus's name.

Family Birthdays: Add to your celebration a time where each family member prays out loud a simple prayer thanking God for the birthday person's life and role in the family. Ask God to bless them in the coming year.

obedience to God and diligence in doing what He asked of them, God paved the way for them to obtain what was promised them.

We decided that our family would do our own "Jericho march" around Annie's new elementary school and around the high school where I would be teaching and our son would be attending the pre-K program on campus.

We each moistened our fingers with olive oil and then walked single file around the perimeter of each school, silently praying for the administrators, the teachers, the students and their families, asking God for protection and blessing, and for our family's interaction among them to be anointed and a blessing to them. As we prayerfully walked the perimeter of the school buildings, we would purposefully anoint the doorposts, marking a small cross over each door with the oil on our fingers.

Of course, we could have stayed in our living room and prayed, and God would have heard. But our kids tell us that they would look up during the school year and see the barely perceptible cross over the door and be encouraged by the memory of the prayers surrounding their school.

As the years went by, we continued our march at each campus where one of us taught or studied. As our children became adolescents, they had some feelings of embarrassment and hoped that no one would see them walking around the building, but no one suggested giving up the tradition.

By our son's sophomore year in high school, the same school where I teach here in San Antonio, he had marched and prayed for his classmates on their various campuses 13 times, and for that particular campus 13 times as well. As we came in our march to the flagpole at the center of the campus, for the first time in 13 years, he broke the silence, and began to pray aloud: "Father, I ask you for a mighty outpouring of your presence here. Lord, I ask that you would cause salvation to spring up from this ground."

The next year, a record 250 students gathered there for See You at the Pole, an annual nationwide event in which students and others are encouraged to gather informally for prayer at their campus flagpole. At the end of the prayertime, Matt said, "If you are here this morning, and you want to ask God to come into your heart, and be a part of your life for the first time, you can come up here, and we [some fellow Christian students] will talk to you and pray with you." As more than 30 kids simultaneously surged forward that day, and then, as the number of students who made first-time professions of faith rose to more than 100 on that public school campus over the next two years, I was often reminded of my son's flagpole prayer. I saw clearly that those somewhat awkward trudges in the August heat and humidity had served a holy purpose beyond our imaginations!

Another tradition that enriched our family life grew out of the True Love Waits program in which our church youth group participated. Greg and I bought each of our kids a chastity ring and presented it in a family ceremony, where the other three family members read letters we had written affirming our faith in that person and in God in them, pledging to protect and support their decision to remain sexually pure until marriage.

What a joy it was to see our daughter give that ring as a symbol to her husband on their wedding day. Now, as the wife of a youth pastor, when she speaks to teenagers about sexual purity she refers to our family ceremony as an altar of commitment in her life. To me, it proves once again that God's principles for designing worship and teaching His ways in our homes are timeless and as effective today as they ever have been.

Through wisdom is an house builded; and by understanding it is established: And by knowledge shall the chambers be filled with all precious and pleasant riches.
—Proverbs 24:3–4 (KJV)

Each of our family traditions becomes one of these treasures, and this is the promise we claim as we seek to make our homes rich in worship.

Stone upon Stone

What spiritual traditions do you remember from your childhood home? Do you still carry on any of those traditions? Why or why not?

What spiritual traditions have you developed in your family over the years?

Looking over an entire year, what seasons or occasions could be enriched by including an activity of spiritual significance?

How would your family benefit from establishing traditions of worship?

One day Jesus was praying in a certain place. When he finished, one of his disciples said to him, "Lord, teach us to pray."
—Luke 11:1

11

Teach Us to Pray

Greg explains how hearing someone pray creates a hunger inside of us, and why worshipping God is all about drawing near to Him. Martha challenges families to stretch their prayer life by offering some focused ideas for intercession.

The more I try to analyze prayer, the more confused I get. I fully understand the importance of prayer. It's more than an obligation. Prayer is more than a discipline. We are created to communicate with God. In fact, one of the reasons God created us is so that He could share intimate fellowship with us. Prayer is the way that He arranged to connect with us on that level. But why prayer? And exactly what's supposed to happen when we pray?

Jesus's disciples were hungry to share in that fellowship, to satisfy the longing for communication with their Creator (Luke 11). Maybe they were a lot like we are. Deep within each individual a desire for more of God cries out to be filled. Sometimes, though, our very best efforts at prayer seem completely inadequate. So we begin a quest for fulfillment that usually includes a series of "prayer calisthenics." Pray more. Pray louder. Pray silently. Pray daily. Pray more consistently. Pray more precisely. Pray more deeply. Pray more conversationally. Pray without ceasing. The solutions and instructions are endless. They are also tiring, stressful, and confusing. There's certainly nothing wrong with any of the efforts, but it usually follows that we get so wrapped up in the *doing* that we miss out on the *being*—the pleasure of fellowship with our Father.

I've never met anyone who told me that they felt they had arrived when it comes to prayer. Not one person has ever told me, "I think I pray just about enough." In fact, I'm certain that

Fast and Feast Together

The practice of fasting and prayer is a valid and effective means by which we focus our prayer life and align our hearts with God's heart. Consider these verses:

Fasting and prayer as a spiritual discipline:

"When you fast, do not look somber as the hypocrites do, for they disfigure their faces to show men they are fasting. I tell you the truth, they have received their reward in full. But when you fast, put oil on your head and wash your face, so that it will not be obvious to men that you are fasting, but only to your Father, who is unseen; and your Father, who sees what is done in secret, will reward you."
—Matthew 6:16–18

Fasting and prayer for protection:

There, by the Ahava Canal, I [Ezra] proclaimed a fast, so that we might humble ourselves before our God and ask him for a safe journey for us and our children, with all our possessions.
—Ezra 8:21

Fasting and prayer for health issues:

David pleaded with God for the child. He fasted and went into his house and spent the nights lying on the ground.
—2 Samuel 12:16

Fasting and prayer for ministry:

While they were worshiping the Lord and fasting, the Holy Spirit said, "Set apart for me Barnabas and Saul for the work to which I have called them." So after they had fasted and prayed, they placed their hands on them and sent them off . . . .

Paul and Barnabas appointed elders for them in each church and, with prayer and fasting, committed them to the Lord, in whom they had put their trust.
—Acts 13:2–3; 14:23

(continued)

if you asked Christians what their greatest spiritual need is, most would reply that it has something to do with an inadequate prayer life. It seems like everyone feels a need to obligate more time to prayer or to realize a greater depth in his or her prayer life. Every believer desires to pray effectively, to gain insight into what to pray about and who to pray for.

Setting Up Stones

Obviously, Jesus's disciples sensed too that prayer was very important to their well-being and that they needed to refine their efforts. When they heard Jesus pray, something stirred within them. They were attracted to the intimacy of His conversation with His Father. It seemed appropriate that they turn to Him to teach them how to achieve the same connection, the same power, and the same reality that was so evident when He talked with God. When they heard Jesus pray, they witnessed the perfect example of what that communication with God was supposed to be like, and they knew that that was what they wanted.

It's certainly not unlike the process that you and I have often experienced. We're hungry for more. We sincerely desire to know God more and share His heart and His desires. Our hearts want to move to even deeper depths each time we experience one of those God moments. "Lord, teach us to pray!"

God's Desire: Draw Near

I suspect that prayer seems so difficult to grasp only because we've made it that way. It's possible our cultural mind-set builds up those walls. We've heard again and again, "Anything worthwhile is worth working for." So we apply that to our spiritual life, and in doing so, we create an internal attitude that replies, *Then if prayer is that good for me, it's going to take a whole lot of work to get it right.* But prayer is not really like that at all.

Just think about it. God wants to have fellowship with us, so He created prayer as the method of achieving that. There's no reason that He would mask it or create a riddle about how it can happen, since He wants it to happen even more than we do. Since He desires fellowship with us, He's certainly not going to run and hide when we take steps in His direction. It's possible that when the disciples asked Jesus to teach them to pray, He might have even been surprised at their request, considering His level of communication with His Father was so profound that it was at the core of His personhood.

Jesus first answered them with the most basic of prayers as a guideline. Then, He proceeded to tell them an uncomplicated story about the relationship between a father and a child.

"Don't bargain with God. Be direct. Ask for what you need. This is not a cat-and-mouse, hide-and-seek game we're in. If your little boy asks for a serving of fish, do you scare him with a live snake on his plate? If your little girl asks for an egg, do you trick her with a spider? As bad as you are, you wouldn't think of such a thing—you're at least decent to your own children. And don't you think the Father who conceived you in love will give the Holy Spirit when you ask him?"

—Luke 11:10–13 *(The Message)*

The Father wants to hear from His children. He wants the conversation to be genuine and from the heart. Intimacy never makes our Father uncomfortable. In fact, it's the very thing that, to Him, reflects what the relationship is all about. Consider these verses:

Dealing with War and Other Disasters

With the increase in terrorism and threats in our world, our children, no matter what their ages, are prey to deeper fears than most of us knew growing up. When a disturbing news report comes on, gather the family and lead them in prayer...for safety, for peace of mind and spirit, for wisdom and protection for leaders, for those dealing first-hand with the crisis, and for direction on how each of you might help. Teach your children that the response to every one of life's situations is to pray and to worship the Father.

Sometimes, the disaster does not make the evening news—it may not even be a true disaster—but it is a big deal to your children. Be sensitive to your kids' reactions to circumstances in their own lives and respond in the same prayerful manner. A lunchroom slight, not making the team, the death of a beloved pet...these, too, are moments when the family should come together to bring those trials before the Lord.

*Let us **draw near** with a true heart in full assurance of faith, having our hearts sprinkled from an evil conscience and our bodies washed with pure water.*
—Hebrews 10:22 (NKJV; emphasis added)

*But it is good for me to **draw near** to God; I have put my trust in the Lord GOD, that I may declare all Your works.*
—Psalm 73:28 (NKJV; emphasis added)

***Draw near** to God and He will **draw near** to you.*
—James 4:8 (NKJV; emphasis added)

It's all about getting closer. You get to know someone by spending time with them. Put aside all the rules and principles you've learned about prayer, and simply talk to God.

Brother Lawrence was an uneducated French layman who lived in the seventeenth century. During a stint in the army as a young man, he experienced a transforming encounter with God. He later went to live in a Carmelite

Praying for Each Other

 Let family members write prayer requests on small slips of paper and then use magnets to place them on the refrigerator door, where other family members can see them and pray.

Pray Without Ceasing

Here are a few ideas that could make your family's prayer life alive and vibrant!

 On small cards or strips of paper have each family member write out a prayer. Place the written prayers in a bowl or basket, and each morning, let the youngest draw one. Have another one read the prayer as you all agree together.

  Occasionally read out loud as a group or do a responsive reading of some of the great prayers of the church, like the Lord's Prayer or the Prayer of St. Francis.

  Encourage individual members of the family to keep their own prayer journals or keep a family prayer journal, where you record what you pray about each day.

  Keep an ongoing list of specific prayer requests, for people outside the family as well as for yourselves, posted on the fridge or some other high-traffic place. As each prayer is answered, mark it with a symbol that indicates that God has answered. Every now and then, as a family, use the list of answered prayers to write a thank-you letter to God.

monastery, where he served primarily in the kitchen. There, in the midst of his steadfast dedication to knowing and serving God, he cultivated a closeness to his heavenly Father, the story of which continues to impact people even today. He said, "There is not in the world a kind of life more sweet and delightful, than that of a continual conversation with God. Those only can comprehend it who practice and experience it." (Brother Lawrence's life and wisdom inspired the Christian classic, *The Practice of the Presence of God*.)

That ongoing conversation with God produces the kind of intimacy that the disciples longed for when they heard Jesus pray. It creates a hunger for more. When your family hears you pray, it models not only our means of communicating with God, but also the depth of the relationship itself.

Kyle Lake was our son's college pastor, mentor, and friend. At the age of 33, he passed away. In that relatively short lifetime, though, he achieved an intimacy with God and a comprehension of prayer that few of us ever reach. He got it. In *ReUnderstanding Prayer* he explains:

> If we want more from our lives with God, we could forge new territory. Terrain that's not readily covered. We could allow prayer to develop fully into what it's already becoming—the fluid, seamless, open-ended conversation with God that threads our day. Conversation that is truly con-versation. "Con" meaning "together" or "with," "verse" meaning "to familiarize by study or experience." So experientially familiarizing ourselves with God. Not to God but with God. Becoming fully present with our unfinished, nonrehearsed thoughts and feelings and allowing God's presence and perspective there. Even amidst the most disjointed, awkward ramblings that lack melody or rhythm.
> —Kyle Lake, *ReUnderstanding Prayer*

Be Real in Prayer

When our family hears our genuine heart for God, they are attracted to it. They want it, too. They learn to pray, not by instructions or memorized verses, but by hearing how we talk to God. It's much more than a pattern being established or an example being followed. Vocalized praying reflects the reality of a close relationship with God. And what a liberating prospect that is! Weeping or laughter, fulfillment or disappointment, can be expressed within that context without taking any thought as to what we might look like or sound like at that moment.

At first, we might be a bit self-conscious in cracking the door to our conversations with God. And, certainly, there are occasions in which it is appropriate to keep our prayer private. But, we should develop a comfort level in praying out loud, in front of our family, so they can witness the closeness of our relationship with Him, and the course that our spiritual journey takes. Our children are not only taught, but are reassured by experiencing that. Out-loud prayers in the home establish that God is real and alive and in control.

Thy Will Be Done

Teach your children to actively seek God's will and pray about their futures.

  When you pass through a town with a college or university, take a moment to drive through campus or get out and take a walk. As you take your tour, discuss with your kids that they may be going to college one day. Talk about all the possibilities in life, and discuss how you know God's leading and direction.

 Make it a point to pray out loud for each of your children's future spouses and encourage them to do the same.

Though Martha's parents took her to church, and honored God and biblical principles in their home, Martha does not recall ever hearing either of her parents pray aloud, beyond a short bedtime prayer or mealtime blessing. So, as a child, she was given no window through which to observe the intimacy of each parent's walk with God. Certain that both of her parents were followers of Jesus, they were nevertheless so private about it that Martha had no sense of what characterized either parent's relationship with Jesus, from what drew them to Him in the first place to what motivated them to continue in their faith until death. Later, as an adult, Martha initiated conversations and asked questions of her mother, but because her father died when she was in her teens, Martha was never able to hear from him the story of his life with God. She missed out on the formative experience of growing in intimacy with God through observing those closest to her.

Where Two or Three Are Gathered

Occasionally, call the family together for a special prayer meeting. This is especially effective when there is a need in the family or with friends. Explain the need and then let family members sit, kneel, stand, pace . . . whatever is comfortable, as they pray out loud together to God. Do not be surprised to sense His presence in your midst, and do not be surprised at how He moves: "Call unto me, and I will answer thee, and show thee great and mighty things, which thou knowest not" (Jeremiah 33:3 KJV).

Set a precedent that any family member may call for a family prayer meeting at any time, and everyone who is available will come.

So what should our children hear us pray about? What's on our mind? What's in our heart? What are we facing? What has God brought us through? Are there decisions to be made? If our objective is to rightly and purely reflect our growing closeness to God, then avoiding these deep issues isn't genuine. Never forget, of course, that what we expose our children to in any context must be age appropriate. But, keeping that in mind, be assured that our many struggles can actually become powerful faith builders for our family as God intervenes. When they hear us pray about good things, hurtful things, disturbing things, or needful things, our kids become aware of God's ever-present connection with us.

Talking to the Creator of the universe, who just happens to be our Father? Wow! That should be exciting! And it will become the most rewarding journey your children will experience when you lead them there confidently and enthusiastically.

Stone upon Stone

When do you pray together as a family? What is the content and focus of those prayers together?

Do you freely share your personal needs with the rest of the family?

Do you ever hear each other's prayers?

Is prayer your first response to a need in your family?

Do you regularly pray for others outside your family?

How can you establish prayer as a natural practice for your family?

Setting Up Stones

So let us celebrate the festival, not with the old bread of wickedness and evil, but with the new bread of sincerity and truth.
—1 Corinthians 5:8 (NLT)

12

Adding Fuel to the Fire

Has your family's passion for God been quenched by the mundane duties of life? Martha presents some heartwarming ideas to bring some sizzle and spark into your home, while also insuring that *all* your kids can know what bacon tastes like!

Preach the word! Be ready in season and out of season.
—2 Timothy 4:2 (NKJV)

The term *family worship* sometimes conjures up visions of Mom and Dad holding everyone captive while they read long passages of begats from the Old Testament, and the children restlessly pinch and poke each other under the table. That's not the picture of worship in the home we've been painting so far, but even the best plans sometimes don't turn out as expected.

My distant cousin's family would gather their four boys at the table every morning for Bible reading and prayer before breakfast. One summer, Mark, a middle brother, visited his grandmother all by himself. Planning for a special breakfast, she asked him, "Mark, do you like bacon with your pancakes?"

"I don't know, Grandma. I've never had any," was his reply.

"Mark!" his grandmother exclaimed. "I know your mother cooks bacon almost every morning!"

"Yeah," he said, "but every morning Jody [who else but the baby brother?] eats it all while Daddy's praying."

And who hasn't called the household together for family worship, only to have six telemarketers phone, the children immediately start fighting, and the delivery guy show up at the door with a package to be signed for?

Fanning the Flames of Faith

As we have seen in the story of Joshua, opportunities for family worship come when we create curiosity in our kids about what it means to walk intimately with God. Some opportunities come as a natural outgrowth of our children observing our own worship. "Can I sing that song with you, Mommy?" "Daddy, why did you have tears when you prayed?" But other

Infusing the Daily with the Divine

The basic goal here is to infuse the daily with the divine. Once you get started, you will find each day full of moments that can be transformed into altars of worship! Here are a few ideas:

 Take a walk around the block, collecting leaves, blossoms, rocks, shells... When you get home, have the kids arrange them, and then explain what each shows about God: His creativity, variety, artistry, humor, and detail.

 Shoot free throws, or play H-O-R-S-E, but before each shot, recite a different Bible verse about a chosen topic. (i.e., God is faithful; Our words are powerful; He is our provider.)

 As a family, write a rap song (or choose another style) about something God has done for you or something about His nature for which you worship Him.

 Love your neighbor as yourself. Anonymously mow the lawn, leave a batch of cookies, rake the leaves...

 Observe Lent in your home (even if this is not your religious tradition) by having each person serve another family member in some way throughout the season.

 Work together as a family to make your outdoor Christmas decorations convey the true meaning of the season—Jesus born for us. Be a blessing to your neighborhood.

(continued)

Setting Up Stones

opportunities are specifically planned. Our families need regular, planned times of worship, daily, weekly, and yearly.

Establishing an effective time of daily family worship can be overwhelming, especially if our expectations are out of sight. Unlike the great prophets and evangelists, we should not expect fire to fall every morning after breakfast.

What we want to do, instead, is build a fire that will burn in steady worship of God for a lifetime in each of our children. A fire such as that is purposefully laid: sparking tinder, slowly adding leaves, then twigs, strategically placing sticks, then small logs, carefully fanning the flames, until at last it is time to add the big log that burns all night. The fire that becomes our sacrifice of praise on the altar of worship is engineered in such a way and grows as days add up to years with our children.

Some basic guidelines for regular family worship include:

Maintain realistic expectations. This planned, daily meeting with God is a time for basic instruction and modeling, for "seed planting." We are setting ourselves up for disappointment and discouragement to view it any other way.

Keep it age-specific. Everyone participates. As you plan, remember that the verse, the presentation, and/or the activity need to be age specific. An effective devotional time for preschoolers is a whole different animal from one that targets your teens. Nevertheless, everyone must be included. If your family is spread out more than a few years, plan to let the older

Infusing the Daily with the Divine

 Teach your children that tithing is an act of worship by helping them set aside one-tenth of their allowance, or other money, with a specific giving goal in mind. For instance, our son-in-law and daughter helped the youth group they lead to raise money for bicycles for an orphanage in Mexico. When they reach that goal and give the money, celebrate!

 When you plan your vacations, look for opportunities to include worship there, too. On a trip through Arkansas, we went to an outdoor production of *The Witness*, a musical passion play, in Hot Springs. Then on a trip to Branson, we drove over to see *The Passion Play* in Eureka Springs. One of the highlights of a trip to New York City was attending the Sunday worship services at *both* Brooklyn Tabernacle and St. Patrick's Cathedral.

 You can buy a new worship CD to listen to in the car or play a Bible trivia game as you ride. Use the uninterrupted time together on the road to tell each other stories of times in your life that display God's faithfulness and provision.

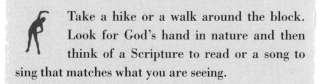 Take a hike or a walk around the block. Look for God's hand in nature and then think of a Scripture to read or a song to sing that matches what you are seeing.

If your heart is set on worshipping God, the opportunities to do so in the midst of day-to-day living are unlimited.

children have a part in leading, or teaching the younger ones. For example, a second-grader might read a simple verse to younger siblings, or help you tell a Bible story. Whatever your situation, keep in mind that the devotion time need not be long.

There is a myriad of devotional books designed for families at all stages of growth. Just stroll through that aisle at your Christian bookstore and choose one that seems comfortable to you.

When our son was a preschooler and our daughter in kindergarten, we used a book that began with a simple Bible verse and then commented very briefly on its application. One morning when Greg was out of town, Matt, trying to be the man of the house, asked if he could lead the devotional, so I handed him the book. He opened the book, glanced at the page, then, in exact imitation of his dad, announced to his sister and me, "The verse this morning is 'Do **not** cross the street.'"

We've laughed at that over the years, but it demonstrates that even at three years old, he had grasped the concept that during our devotion time we were learning important guidelines for how we would conduct our lives.

Family time doesn't replace your own time with God. Be sure that the entire family understands that this is not a replacement for personal prayer and Bible study, but that family "devos," as we say, are a time when we as an entire family declare God's worth and seek to know and follow His ways.

It _is_ possible to find the time. Making devotions a part of the daily family routine is a challenge, especially when we all seem to be so busy with school, church, sports, music lessons, dentist appointments, and a thousand other important demands on our time and attention. It seems rare to find a family that can manage one meal a day together, much less a set time for devotions.

Experiment to find a time that fits your family routine, but realize two things. First, an effective family worship time need not take more than 10 to 15 minutes daily, and second, it _is_ a sacrifice that you _choose_ to make.

Accept no substitutes. Families who send their children to Christian schools may be tempted to say, "The kids get enough at school every day; we've got it covered that way." But there is no substitute for that few minutes of study in God's Word, prayer, and praise as a family to impress upon our children that God is real, we walk with Him day by day, and He is a priority in our home.

Beyond the Daily Grind

There are times, though, when more is needed. Often, we call a family meeting in the living room, where as a family, we worship, and as a family, we call out to God for our needs and the needs of others.

Our moments of weakness, of uncertainty, are the perfect opportunity to teach our children that God is faithful and to show them how to live by faith. Rather than hiding potential problems and trials from our kids, trying "to protect them," we ask them to partner with us in prayer . . . and so they get to share our rejoicing as well when, time after time, God demonstrates His sufficiency and faithfulness to us. By approaching worship and prayer as a family, our children learn the practical necessity of our walk with God.

Until our children were both in college, the most treasured family time we spent all year long was probably our annual family retreat, a special weekend where we got away together and spent the entire time focused on worship, Bible study, and prayerfully seeking God as a family.

On other outings, we may have played board games, rented movies, tossed a football, or hiked, but this was a weekend devoted to drawing away as a family and drawing near to God.

When the children were in upper elementary school, and were physically and mentally able to sustain focus over that length of time, we began the weekend retreats as a way to find a unified spiritual direction for the school year ahead. These were not boring weekends for sitting quietly with long faces. They were filled with activity that sparked the kids' interest.

On one, both the kids and Greg and I spent an entire morning working with cardboard, fabric, paper, markers, glitter, ribbon, and glue to create shields that symbolized our family. In the afternoon, we each explained all the symbols on our shields, which led to an open discussion of our individual roles and relationships within the family and how our interactions could honor God and be a blessing to each other. In the evening, we sat around the table, and sentence by sentence, with even the youngest giving input, crafted our family creed. That framed creed remains prominently displayed in our living room, and our four shields grace the wall of our workout-computer-craft-junk room.

Again, as our children matured, the content and activities changed, until finally, the year that both kids were in high school together, they planned the Bible study, the activities, and the schedule, and they led the retreat for *us*. Year after year, that weekend was a spiritual benchmark for the family, because as we made the effort to draw aside and seek Him as a family, God was faithful to honor our efforts by drawing near to us.

Serendipity Strikes Again

But in addition to our deliberate, planned opportunities for worship–daily, weekly, annually–there is another kind of opportunity, the kind I call *serendipity*.

> *These commandments that I give you today are to be upon your hearts. Impress them on your children. Talk about them when you sit at home and when you walk along the road, when you lie down and when you get up.*
> —Deuteronomy 6:7

How to Plan a Family Retreat

 Note the key word: *plan.*

Place: The place could be a cabin, a motel room, a tent...but it needs to be away from the phone, TV, drop-by friends, or any other distractions. This is probably **not** the time to go to Orlando. If you can't swing a weekend, try for at least a full day.

Purpose: The purpose is to draw away to intensely seek God as a family, to learn what He would teach you/ ask of you.

Theme: The parents should spend time seeking the theme, or focus, of the retreat. It might be a subject, such as family relationships or the power of words, or it could be a particular Scripture to study. If you are not comfortable coming up with this on your own, choose from the hundreds of workbooks and lessons available in your Christian bookstore. Pay close attention and select materials appropriate for the median age of your children.

Schedule: This whole thing will fall apart unless you have a schedule, and stick to it! Make it clear that this weekend is not a vacation. You as a family are setting aside this time for a holy purpose!

- Plan for a lesson time, during which you explore the Word. It should be 15 to 20 minutes per session for elementary schoolers, 30 to 40 minutes for middle schoolers, and 45 to 60 minutes for ages 14 and up.
- Follow this with a directed activity, which allows for consideration/application of the lesson: It could be an art or craft project to illustrate the lesson, a scavenger hunt or nature walk, a game, an original skit...Whatever you come up with, parents and kids participate together, on an equal level.
- Plan time for both family and individual prayer, meditation, worship, and devotion. This might be a good chance to use the CD player and play some worship music or to have family members play instruments.
- Meals should be simple, with everyone helping with preparation and cleanup.
- In the evening, you can sing by the fireside or starlight, share stories, or play a game or do an activity that fits with the day's theme.
- Plan for one activity that allows your family members to create something that will serve as a reminder of the retreat...an art or craft project, a family-made video, a piece of writing, and so forth.

Tip: Just this one time a year, allow no free time—no fishing, swimming, playing sports or spades or board games. Keep every moment, every activity, centered and focused on seeking God together as a family.

We have to be on the alert for Deuteronomy 6:7 moments, or we'll miss opportunities to talk of God's commandments when we sit in our houses, when we walk by the way, when we lie down, and when we get up. These serendipitous times of worship, perhaps most precious because they are unplanned, grow out of habits of family worship that we have purposefully developed, but they are triggered by our heartfelt responses to situations we find ourselves in unexpectedly.

The prompt may be a news story that leads to a family discussion, when talk turns to what God's Word says about the subject, or it could be a chance comment that a family member makes on the drive to the grocery store. I was amazed to read, in an email my baby sister sent only recently, that her great fear of storms as a child had been put to rest one evening when we stood in our garage together watching thunderstorms sweep across the Texas Panhandle. At the time, she was 9, and I was 19, and I had no idea of the depth of her fear. But, I began to sing the lines from "How Great Thou Art": "I hear the rolling thunder/ Thy power throughout the universe displayed . . ." That simple moment of open response to God's creation was a life-changing moment for a 9-year-old, but I wasn't to know it until we both had teenagers of our own!

On a family vacation to Estes Park, Colorado, we were driving through the park at about sundown one evening, when we noticed a number of elk drinking water from a pond in a green valley surrounded by mountains. We pulled off the road to enjoy the sight, made even more beautiful by the extravagant sunset reflecting in the pool. As we silently watched, Annie, who was 13 at the time, began to sing the worship chorus, "As the Deer," based on Psalm 42:1, "As the deer pants for the water brooks, So pants my soul for You, O God" (NKJV). After only a few notes, the rest of the family joined in, and we sat in our car, worshipping God together, until the stars began to appear. We have forgotten many details of that two-week trip, but that moment stands out vividly for each of us as a highlight of our vacation in Colorado.

Seizing every opportunity to worship as a family creates heart habits that enrich our individual intimacy with God for all of our lives. While we may feel unequal to the task of designing set devotion times or shy about being the first to respond to a spiritual moment with words of worship or a song, we can be encouraged knowing that God will honor our efforts, however inadequate, every time.

Stone upon Stone

What do you generally focus your thoughts and conversation on during the course of your day?

In your family, what times daily do you spend interacting with each other? What is the focus of your thoughts and conversation during those times? What are some ways you could shift the focus toward God?

How would a change of focus change your home?

What activity could you plan for one day next week that would create a natural opportunity for your family to think and talk about God?

Joshua set up the twelve stones that had been in the middle of the Jordan at the spot where the priests who carried the ark of the covenant had stood. And they are there to this day.
—Joshua 4:9

13

And the Stones Remain to This Day

What's up with Greg's sore feet? And which little Scripture causes so much angst? Meanwhile, Martha uses a story about growing up in the Texas Panhandle to model a fresh way to create something monumental.

The last sentence of Joshua 4:9 seems to be an almost insignificant addendum unless you take notice of it and begin to meditate upon it—*"And they are there to this day."* This note actually refers to a second memorial of stones built by Joshua in the middle of the Jordan River, mirroring the one set up by the families in their camp. In any case, whether the arrangement still stands today or not isn't important—the verse isn't intended to speak about the engineering genius of Joshua and his men. Instead, I think this verse is in Scripture to remind us of the eternal truths that the tribes of Israel took care to pass on to the generations that followed them. Those stones still speak of a people's obedience and their God's faithfulness. They reveal the heart of the heavenly Father, what His priorities are, and what He considers eternally significant.

What was so special about these two piles of rocks? It surely wasn't the way they were set up. Why was it important that the men brought a rock into their camp (homes)? Certainly, the effort wasn't made simply for the purpose of safekeeping.

One of God's primary, eternal desires is to connect with people. In the Garden of Eden, God anticipated His daily fellowship with Adam and Eve. He structured time and setting precisely so they could be together. Then, when sin separated mankind from God, He set in motion a purposeful plan to restore we who were lost. The stones Joshua and his men set up were special reminders in the unfolding history of redemption, which would reach its crucial point in Christ's death and resurrection, and continues today as He calls people from every nation to Him. As such, the stones represent God's faithfulness and his desire to have a relationship with us.

I never liked those plastic building blocks. They appear to be innocent enough, hard-plastic, raw materials intended for the amusement of curious and creative children. I'm fairly certain, though, that, despite their innocuously inanimate appearance, they must be alive. They are nocturnal creatures that have sought to inflict pain upon me, particularly upon my feet. How else could they have always managed to be on the floor of my kids' bedrooms in the middle of the night? Those precious little children wouldn't actually leave them out on purpose, would they? Like traversing a minefield, I sought to negotiate my way through Anne's and Matt's bedrooms in our dark house. My feet always found those little instruments of torture. I can assure you, it's nearly impossible to remain in that stealthy don't-wake-the-kids mode with hard plastic blocks penetrating the soles of your feet.

As much as I despised them, our kids loved them. And as a result, their rooms were full of them. There was always an impressive structure under construction, surrounded by collateral building materials. When the lights were on, they returned to their original state, and, then, I couldn't help but appreciate the formidable structures that my children had designed.

God has presented to us and our families serendipities and events that we can use like building blocks to create something meaningful. He gave instructions for constructing memories and building connections. The spiritual structure we create in our families is a legacy, a history, that points back toward Him. Certain stones in the structure speak about significant events in our lives, when He proved His love or His faithfulness to us. Some stones are simple things, everyday occurrences that we have observed carefully and in which we have found Him there, showing us His desire for us to know Him more. And some of the stones are biblical truths, building a foundation as He constantly reveals His never-changing character.

A Fresh Look at Proverbs 22:6

If it weren't for the fact that it is a powerful portion of God's Word, I think that by now I would almost be weary of hearing all about Proverbs 22:6.

> *Train a child in the way he should go, and when he is old he will not turn from it.*
> —Proverbs 22:6

So much study, so much teaching, so much rhetoric has been dispensed from this theme. It has been used to encourage, to chastise, and to caution. We've been told it guarantees everything, and it guarantees nothing. Many parents have wept over it, while many rejoiced in it.

I've seen too many godly, well-meaning parents who diligently raised their children to find God only to have one of them stray from the faith. I've caught myself wondering, *Where did they go wrong? Are they, perhaps, not the kind of parents they seem to be?* And, sometimes then, I even sought to discount them or even disqualify them in the light of Proverbs 22:6. But I never felt right about having that kind of judgmental attitude. I feared there was something very wrong in my viewpoint. So in light of its misuse and misinterpretation, including sometimes my own, I have sought to discover a balanced, correct interpretation of this verse that can be embraced as a pragmatic promise.

The facts are irrefutable. We can do most things right in the way we teach our kids about our faith, and there is still a chance that they will reject it. I can't tell you for certain what we did that worked in our family. We made a lot of mistakes. There were many times I did or said things that didn't in the least reflect Christ to my children. It humbles me to know, though, that in spite of those mistakes, God in His grace made a powerful connection with them. I'm just so thankful that both our children, now in their 20s, have a vital, dynamic faith in God, and have joined us as true worshippers on the journey that is abundant life.

I have come to a realization that, though parents can be the conduits that introduce their child to a genuine relationship with Christ and they can encourage their child in true worship, it's ultimately between God and the child. We should continue to model true worship, and at every opportunity, point out "God at work." But, we can never *make* it happen. That's not even our responsibility.

A closer look at Proverbs 22:6 does reveal a few clear guidelines that can perhaps give us something more concrete to build upon.

Each "way" is different. There's something I love about math. Before you get the idea that formulas are my forte, you should know that I approach algebra, geometry, calculus, and even simple addition and subtraction from a whole other side of the brain. But I do love the fact that there is so much order to it. It's so logical.

Wouldn't it be nice if I could produce for you a single rule or procedure that, if followed to the letter, would assure that your child would become a true worshipper? A neat package, complete with clear, explicit directions would be ideal. The fact is, it doesn't work that way at all. Each child is unique so the proper approach is as varied as the number of children in the history of mankind.

The only rule is that every child's "way" is different. That's why building an altar in the hearts of your children requires diligent observation and investigation. Not everything you do will connect. It might connect with one of your kids but not the other, possibly with

From Caprock to Ebenezer Garden

When I was growing up in the Texas Panhandle, my best friend, Patty, lived on a big ranch 20 miles from town. It was always a wonderful treat to get to visit the ranch, and Patty and her older brother and sister often had friends out for the weekend. About five miles before we reached the ranch house, a long, skinny bridge of land led from the dirt road out to the top of a mesa-like formation that fell away sharply on all sides. People from anywhere other than the flatlands of Oklahoma, Kansas, or Nebraska would not be impressed, but in the flat, treeless landscape of the Texas Panhandle, that land formation, with the series of canyons and arroyos that cut through the grasslands behind it, was a real landmark.

We called it the "caprock." Patty's family had a tradition that every time anyone visited their ranch for the first time, they pulled off the road, and led the newcomer carefully across the "bridge" (keeping a careful eye out for rattlesnakes!) to place their own rock on the substantial pile of stones already atop the caprock. So, these stones came to represent each friend who had visited there.

The caprock, with its four-foot pile of rocks on top, was the landmark we used to keep our bearings as we roamed the ranch on horses or on foot. On the last weekend before our group of friends dispersed for our various colleges, it was the place we chose to say our formal good-byes.

In many ways, it was an altar of remembrance for friendships and experiences shared over 12 years growing up together. Although 40 years have passed, and the ranch is no longer in the same family, whenever I return to my hometown, what I most want to do is drive out once again to see the caprock, to revisit treasured memories of people and events from childhood.

That experience, coupled with our study from Joshua, inspired our family to make an "Ebenezer garden." The word *ebenezer*, first referred to in 1 Samuel 4, means "stone of help," and the idea of the garden is to mark the moments of God's grace that occur in each of our journeys.

(continued)

ou never know when, or even if,
eep on trying. You continue to try
reading from a book of devotions
es of life, colored by lessons that
n his or her own path.

How old is the child referred to
orship when our child develops a
ough to a teenager? Once a son or
e? The "child" to whom Proverbs
anslated "offspring." And, that is
son to season in the life of a child,
pon us for every detail of life, to
e her independence, and into her
d counsel when it's sought, we're
d caring for any brother or sister
unending.

altars for our family never ends.
as true worshippers, I still must
y Father. As another believer on
strength and inspiration to them.
ically, I still have a responsibility
ce, counsel, and, above all else,

hildren in worship is a task that
-out. We never earn a break. The
cious for that. We must constantly
elevant ways.

ts in the spiritual atmosphere in
strating and hurtful. Proverbs 22
our children into worshippers are
hazy for us. We wouldn't have to
hat formula was in place in which
result, then we would be tireless
ard would be all we would need to

Spirit is doing to draw our entire
self known through circumstances
imately it's not our responsibility

to make all our efforts work. Our understanding is that when we do what God is asking of us, we can believe that He is at work to bring the result that we hope for. Hebrews 11 is the great chapter of faith that is foundational in our relationship with God. It defines what this faith in Him is all about.

> *Faith is the confidence that what we hope for will actually happen; it gives us assurance about things we cannot see.*
> —Hebrews 11:1 (NLT)

Never give up on God! He's at work when we're weary of the unchanged circumstances, when we don't see the results we hope for, and when we feel like we can't take another step. God works independently of circumstances and appearances. Of course, small victories that point toward the right direction are always a source of encouragement. And God often works that way. But we should always recall that God isn't confined to working gradually, step-by-step. Remember Saul of Tarsus? He was the reviled persecutor of early Christians. He was on his way to Damascus when God stepped in. In a single miraculous moment, Saul, the murderer, became Paul, the apostle who changed the world with Christ's message.

Ultimately, as I've written earlier, we cannot force a relationship between our children

From Caprock to Ebenezer Garden

Here's how to make your own:

Start by choosing a spot in the yard—an existing flower bed, the sides of a walkway, anywhere that seems appropriate to you—to start your Ebenezer garden.

For both the family as a whole and each member separately, every time God answers a specific prayer or demonstrates His grace in a special way, pick out a rock, and using a permanent marker, write on the rock a word or phrase that signifies the event. Include the person's name (if an individual family member) and the date, and place the rock in the garden. If rocks are hard to come by where you live, you can purchase smooth river rocks.

As the collection of rocks grows, it will serve as a call to faith and a reminder of God's goodness and specific grace to your family. As you occasionally look over your Ebenezer garden, you will be reminded that the first call to each of us is to cultivate hearts that worship.

And as you nurture habits of worship in your family, those will be passed to the next generation, as well. I like to imagine grandchildren examining those rocks and asking to hear the stories of adventures in faith from their parents, grandparents, uncles, and aunts.

When we purpose in our hearts to set up stones in our homes that call our children's hearts to worship, we can be assured that, like those placed by Joshua, the stones will remain to succeeding days.

and God. Each child's vital, vibrant walk with God is between him or her and the Lord. God's role for us as parents is to build the altars where our children can discover Him.

Building altars requires a purposeful plan. A careless arrangement of the stones won't last. We can't just allow them to lie right where we uncovered them and expect something eternal to happen. We can't simply toss them in a pile hoping that maybe they'll fall in a way that creates something significant or meaningful. We have to meticulously set up those stones. All the building blocks that God provides for us need to be examined and carefully analyzed. Then, we must determine how and where we use them so they will be most effective. Our work must be purposeful and intentional.

Finally, as a result of all the effort, we'll discover we've actually built an altar. In our home, we will have prepared a place where our family can worship God wholeheartedly and genuinely. The stones of this altar are laughter and tears, victories and struggles, lessons learned, a legacy of faith, songs of praise and victory, and stories that reflect God's love and power. By being diligent and deliberate we have arranged them into an altar—a place where God's character is revealed and His name is exalted!

Stone upon Stone

Are circumstances in your home, like busyness, dictating whether or not God is a part of your daily lives?

Have you let the perceived success or failure of previous attempts cause you to give up your efforts in making home a place of worship?

How could changing your approach to "setting up stones" in your home change the way worship works there?

What daily activities around your home do you see becoming opportunities for worship?

How determined are you in your attempt to create an atmosphere of worship in your home? Do you believe your diligence matters?

Activity Index

Creative Arts

Performing Arts

Physical Activity

Service Activity

Reading

Bible Focus

Prayer Focus

Prayer Focus, *continued from p. 157*

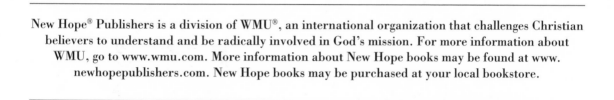

New Hope® Publishers is a division of WMU®, an international organization that challenges Christian believers to understand and be radically involved in God's mission. For more information about WMU, go to www.wmu.com. More information about New Hope books may be found at www.newhopepublishers.com. New Hope books may be purchased at your local bookstore.

More Parenting Resources

from New Hope

Missions Moments 2
*52 Easy-to-Use Missional
Messages and Activities for
Today's Family*
Mitzi Eaker
ISBN: 1-59669-210-3

Families on Mission
*Ideas for Teaching
Your Preschooler to Love,
Share, and Care*
Angie Quantrell
ISBN: 1-56309-991-8

Mommy Pick-Me-Ups
*Refreshing Stories
to Lighten Your Load*
Edna Ellison and Linda Gilden
ISBN: 1-59669-218-9

Baby Boot Camp
*Basic Training for the First
Six Weeks of Motherhood*
Rebecca Ingram Powell
ISBN: 1-56309-820-2

Available in bookstores everywhere

For information about these books or any New Hope product, visit www.newhopepublishers.com.